Ple:

Long Way Back

CHARLEY BOORMAN

Long Way Back

with Jeff Gulvin

Published by AA Publishing, a trading name of AA Media Limited,
Fanum House, Basing View, Basingstoke, Hampshire RG21 4EA, UK.
shop.theAA.com

First published in 2017. This paperback edition published 2018.
10 9 8 7 6 5 4 3 2

A CIP catalogue record for this book is available from the British Library

ISBN: 978-0-7495-7925-8

Editors: Rebecca Needes and Charlotte Lester
Art Director: James Tims
Cover Design: Two Associates and Tom Whitlock
Cover Photographer: Peter Beavis

Typeset in Bembo Regular 11pt

Printed and bound by CPI Group (UK) Ltd, Croydon, CR0 4YY
A05649

This is for Olivia, Doone and Kinvara

my angels

CONTENTS

FOREWORD

I was about to get my motorbike out of the garage when the text came through from Billy. Having just finished *American Pastoral,* I was up to my neck in post-production, and due at the editing suite. I stopped short, a chill working through me as I read a message from Charley's assistant, telling me he'd come off a motorbike in Portugal.

Immediately I called Charley's cell phone, but it wasn't him that answered. It was somebody else. 'Hello, this is Charley's phone.'

That was ominous.

'Is he there?' I said. 'Can I speak to him? It's Ewan, I'm calling from LA.'

'Ewan, sorry, no, you can't talk to him. This is Nigel from Triumph: he's in the hospital, they're operating on him right now.'

He explained what had happened and it was pretty serious. I told him I'd call back later. I found myself standing there staring at my motorbike, thinking maybe I ought to take the car today. That's how it affects you when a mate is involved in a serious spill; like an omen, it seeps into every pore. I just couldn't believe it; not Charley, not being hit by a car. Charley doesn't get hit by a car: he's too good, too confident, he's always too aware. For 20 years we've been riding together, and most of that he was on the back wheel. I tried to convince myself he'd be OK. We'd had near misses once or twice – I mean Charley almost got wiped out before we left London on the first day of *Long Way Round*. Still it would not sink in. Not Charley: he's invincible. He's always been that way.

I kept thinking how the two of us had ridden 40,000 miles across Europe and Russia, and all the way across America too. We'd ridden right through Africa with lorries coming at us from all directions, overloaded buses swinging round mountain roads, not to mention camels and donkeys, myriad pedestrians crossing in front of us. Not once did either of us have a serious spill. I looked from bike to car and car to bike knowing that I'd take the bike, almost as if it was me who'd come off and I had to get back on right away.

I called Olivia in London and as I waited for her to pick up all I could think about was Charley in the hospital with a shattered leg. I had no idea how long his road to recovery would be…

Ewan McGregor

PART ONE

16 – 24 February 2016:

Algarve, Portugal

PRESS DAY

The morning it happened I was in Portugal on a brand new Triumph Tiger Explorer. I was lagging behind a dozen members of the American press corps, wondering what they would think of the new bike and whether they'd be as positive as the Brits. But if I didn't catch up with them, I wouldn't find out. Shifting my concentration back to the road, I negotiated a twisty section of the EN125 that led through town. Two lanes of blacktop stretched in front of me; I'd left the commercial area behind and was in amongst some spacious-looking houses.

I was pushing on, pushing the new Triumph, still trying to catch up. The sun was low and awkward in the sky, but the traffic was much lighter now that I'd left the more built-up area. I pressed on, passing a bus and a couple of cars, then came up behind a Mercedes. Up ahead there were a couple of large villa-style properties on my right, and I noticed another on the left behind a solid-looking stone wall. That house, with that wall, sat at the junction of the main road and a left-hand turn.

I was alongside the Mercedes – I'd just pulled out to overtake – when the driver suddenly started to drift. My heart was in my mouth, the wing of the car swinging sharply in front of me now; she was making the turn and she hadn't seen me. Desperately, I tried to scrub off speed. My mouth was dry, no trace of saliva. Hard on the brakes. She hadn't seen me. Nowhere to go. Jesus Christ, that wall!

FEET FIRST

That's how my twin sister Daisy made her entrance into this world after forcing me out a few moments before. I swear she shuffled around in the womb to breach on purpose, because nine months is a long time to be stuck with no one to talk to but me.

Actually, my dad says we started speaking late – and that was largely because we had our own language. I can't tell you what that sounded like, it's been 50 years, but we had this way of communicating with each other without really talking and that might've started in the womb.

Mum and Dad were amazed at the way we both seemed to know what was going on and during those early years it was as if we were the only two children in the world. We were inseparable even when we were fighting, though that wasn't very often. We'd play games with each other, try and outdo one another even though we were the best of friends. I remember one time when Daisy was pushing me in a wheelbarrow along this ridge of earth at the back of our house with a patch of stinging nettles growing below. I had no idea what was coming until I was rolling down the bank into the nettles. I couldn't believe it. My sister had tipped me out of the barrow and I was stung so badly that my mum plastered me with dock leaves for weeks.

You know what, though? Now I think about it I might have got it wrong. Memories can be like that; what you think happened and what actually did happen can grow further apart with the repeated telling of the story. Like Chinese Whispers the truth gets blurred, and though I think it was me in the wheelbarrow, it could well have been the other way around. Whichever it was, I write this some 40 years later and both Daisy and I are now 50. I can't believe it. I never thought I'd make it this far. Daisy never thought I would – and after the events in Portugal, I'm lucky to be here at all.

We spilled into the world in Wimbledon on 23 August 1966, not long after England won the World Cup, though that didn't mean anything to us back then. People often talk about the drama and uncertainty of life and for me it was evident right from the get-go. Daisy and I were born into a family that people describe as larger than life. Everything we experienced as children was normal to us of course, and like everyone else we were shaped by the people around us. I had no concept of it being anything but ordinary. Looking back now, I can see it was unconventional: a family led by a maverick movie maker who took on the established order of things, carving a place in history by making two of the most iconic 'American' movies of all time. It's quite a feat for an Englishman to take on Hollywood at their own game.

In 1966 Dad made *Point Blank* with Lee Marvin, and in 1972 he filmed *Deliverance,* where John Voight and Burt Reynolds canoe down an old river in rural Georgia before the valley is flooded. Appalachia, hillbillies, people living on the very fringes of modern America; *Deliverance* has an official place in American cultural history. The movie is often remembered for a young inbred kid playing the banjo and a male rape scene that was unprecedented at the time. In *Point Blank* Dad showed the kind of brutal violence associated with Tarantino, when Quentin was still just a kid. That was his first film with Lee Marvin, a World War II veteran who was wounded in action and knew what real violence was. He knew how to handle a gun and came to prominence with Marlon Brando, riding motorbikes in *The Wild One.* When I spoke to Dad about it recently, he said that Lee told him The Beatles took the name for their band from one of the biker gangs in that film: the 'Beetles'. Whether that's true or not I guess you'd have to ask Paul McCartney.

I've seen that film more times than I care to remember. The first real biker movie ever made, it was based on events that took place during the 4th of July weekend in 1947. A small town (much like the one portrayed in the movie) called Hollister, where an American Motorcyclist Association (AMA) rally turned into a drunken brawl. The events were so sensationalised by the media that the AMA was forced to put out a statement assuring the public that those involved represented less than one per cent of American motorcyclists and no one had anything to fear. The comment backfired badly though, because the one per cent moniker was later adopted by the Hells Angels and other bike gangs such as the Bandidos, Outlaws and Vagos.

I don't know if the fact that Lee Marvin was around so much during my childhood influenced the way I got into bikes or not, but I did know he'd ridden one in that movie. All I know is that something spawned a love of motorbikes that's brought me a life I could never have imagined. It's a life where I've taken risks, both reasonable and unreasonable, and I came through them pretty unscathed.

After that day in Portugal, however, I found myself in the kind of battle I never thought I'd face. Never mind ride a motorbike – I wasn't sure if I'd ever walk properly again.

So the reason I was in Portugal was for the launch of the Tiger Explorer XC, in my new role as a Triumph ambassador. I'd worked with BMW for more than ten years, riding around the world, racing the Dakar Rally on their motorbikes. I had been thinking I needed to try something different when Triumph approached Russ Malkin, my friend and the producer of the *Long Way* series. They wanted me and I wanted them, and when that's how it is, a deal is generally made.

That was in the autumn of 2015. Christmas came and went, the new year settled into February and suddenly I was looking forward to four glorious days of testing the all-new Explorer with a bunch of journalists from all over the world. The time seemed to shift so quickly – but then things happen fast around motorbikes. Especially when you're on a motorbike.

It all started so perfectly. First out were a dozen guys from the UK including Marc Potter and MCN's Neevesy. Flying into Faro, we took a car out to a beautiful hotel and unpacked our gear. Hospitality was great, and I co-chaired a presentation given by the marketing guys where the various facets of the new bike were outlined to the gathered journalists. A little rain had fallen over the weekend and that washed out an off-road section that Triumph had planned to let both the Brits and the American contingent test the bike on. It didn't matter though; that first day was excellent.

I hadn't ridden the new Tiger before and I was amazed at how planted and balanced it felt on the road. It steered superbly and the suspension was incredible, able to sense the weight of the rider and react accordingly. By the time we got back to the hotel that night I was buzzing from the exhilaration of the ride and thinking just how good this new role with Triumph was going to be.

The following morning dawned cold and crisp. The clouds that had hung around the previous day had gone and the sky was the brilliant blue that we'd been hoping for. Having had their turn on the bikes the British journalists would be heading home, and it was the turn of the Americans. I woke up still on a high, seriously impressed with the way the bike had handled and excited to be riding again. The electronics were second to none and the front wheel hoisted with ease. I know I'm bound to be a little biased, but I've always rated the Hinckley outfit and I reckon I'm pretty analytical when it comes to what's good or not as regards motorbikes. For a beefy-looking all-round adventurer the

Tiger was great both on the sweeping bends and in the tighter, more technical corners. There were moments when I was clicking through the gears with the bike cranked over, with every inch of feel I wanted from the front wheel and perfect balance at the rear.

I donned a pair of Kevlar jeans and my favourite Rev-It boots, as well as a brand new jacket and the neck buff I'd saved from *Long Way Down*. I made sure I had a down-filled puffa under the jacket for warmth, then I spoke to my wife on the phone. Olivia and I have been together 30 years and married for 25. She's been with me through thick and thin and she could hear the excitement in my voice. She had stuff to do though, so we kept the conversation brief and then I went outside to the same buzz in the air that I'd experienced the previous day. A sense of adventure and anticipation, the journalists waiting by the bikes for me to demonstrate the electronics and suspension settings so they could set them up as they wanted. When that was sorted, we saddled up and left the car park in convoy.

I was happy. Triumph seemed pretty happy too, and I was already looking forward to riding a Tiger for an extended period in a month or so, when I would lead an expedition from Melbourne to Sydney by way of Tasmania. As we hit the road, though, I realised I'd been so busy showing the Americans how to adjust the suspension settings that I'd neglected to take a look at mine. Pulling over I made a quick tweak, then I was back on the bike and popping a wheelie.

There is nothing that beats being on a motorbike when the day is young and the world is still pulling its boots on.

There's a freshness to the air that you can almost taste; it was my favourite time of day when I made my way through Africa with Ewan McGregor. Maybe it's because there's not too much humidity, but for some reason it's at that time of day that the engine seems at its sweetest.

When I'm away (which is about seven months of every year) I'm always happier when I've spoken to my wife Olivia. Olly's been the rock that's kept me sane(ish) all these years and she's helped guide my career. She's so beautiful that when I first met her I never thought I'd have a chance. We hung out with the same group of friends and I was waiting to pounce – only she disappeared off the scene before I had a chance to ask her out. I was gutted; there one day and gone the next, and nobody seemed to know why she had vanished.

About a year later she popped up at a party I'd been invited to, and when I saw her I knew nothing had changed. I wanted her just as much then as I had before; I was determined to go out with this girl. She was nice enough to me but there was nothing to indicate any romantic notions on her part, so I knew I had to do something to get her to notice me. It wasn't going to be easy. Olly was three years older than me – and at just 20, I wasn't exactly mature. I could tell she liked me, but I got the impression she thought I was a little bit young for her. They say women are far more mature than men anyway and I'm a kid at heart, so it was difficult to get anything going. We had a couple of mutual friends though, so I used them to engineer ways of seeing her. She was working as an estate agent and Jason Connery – Sean's son, a great friend of mine and part of my first-ever motorbike adventure – was looking for a place to buy. Obviously I made sure it was Olly's estate agency he went to. She showed us a couple of places, including one with a bloody great crack in the wall, and needless to say Jason didn't bite. I tried my best but she still didn't seem very interested, but after months of pursuit and wooing she finally agreed to go out on a date.

When we got married five years later Jason was my best man. He'd long since left London for LA, and I always joke that when he did that he left me. He'll tell you it wasn't like that at all – when I met Olly, I left Jason, not the other way around.

Looking back on that time from a hospital bed I thought he might be right: I was obsessed with her. I still am. It took so long to actually get her to go out with me that I was never sure if she wanted to be with me at all. We'd have these moments when we started dating; when the evening was over I'd drop her off and there would be an awkward silence while we tried to figure out if we were going to kiss or not. Then she'd get out of the car and I thought she'd go straight into the house, but as I drove off I'd look in the mirror and she'd still be standing there.

I'm drifting. I'm badly dyslexic; it takes all my time just to read a book, never mind write one. My mind jumps from subject to subject and wanders off all the time.

Portugal. 16 February 2016. The crisp morning. Full of excitement for my new role with Triumph, delighting in the brand new Tiger beneath me, I was out of the main part of town and there wasn't much traffic around, but the sun was reflecting off the buildings and car windows and I knew I had to be mindful.

The bike shifted through the gears like a hot knife through butter, emitting a good old-fashioned rasp from the stainless-steel exhaust. With the active suspension the ride height was perfect both on the straight and in mid-corner. I was messing around, speeding up and slowing down, punching up and down the gearbox to see how it would respond to a bit of pressure. I peeled into the bends, shifting my weight off the seat like a road racer – I stood up on the pegs as if I was riding off road and felt the suspension working again. It was the kind of set-up that immediately gives the rider confidence, and I was beginning to get an idea of what it would be like in the kind of terrain we'd cover in Australia.

But as it turned out, that wasn't going to happen. Australia, the terrain, the trip…I pulled out to overtake that Merc, the driver turned hard left and there was no way I could avoid that wall.

Quite what happened I can't be sure. It seemed to be the faintest of contacts with the car, but the next thing I knew I was flying through the air. I hit the ground with a bone-crunching shudder; in my leg, my hip, my sternum, all the way up to my shoulders. I didn't hit once but twice, three times, and each impact was worse than the last. I've never felt anything like it – the ground coming up to meet me again and again – the reverberation was just incredible. I lay there for a moment trying to find a breath that wasn't there. I was trying not to panic. I was trying not to succumb to the fear.

I could see something from the corner of my eye that I couldn't quite make out until I realised it was a wheel bouncing down the road. It went on and on and I thought: *What the fuck is a wheel doing bouncing down that side road?* I couldn't take it in. Then I saw bits of tank and chassis headed the other way. *God*, I thought, *that's a mess.* And then, as if some other section of my brain re-engaged, I was on the pavement in agony.

The pain was incredible. It surrounded my left knee and I could feel it through my hip. Looking down at my legs I could see that part of the engine (the crankshaft, I think) was underneath. Jesus, I was sitting on the engine of the brand new bike I'd been riding a moment before. I couldn't comprehend it. I knew I'd been airborne because I'd seen the kerb coming up to meet me and thought how much it was going to hurt. And it did. As I sat there a pain was shooting through my leg as if someone was stabbing it with a heated blade. I could feel sweat on my forehead under my helmet; it rolled into my eyes to burn and blind. I sat in shock trying to isolate that pain. I could feel it high in my left buttock and all the way down my thigh.

I was aware of a jarring sensation as well now, and it seemed to shake my entire body. I straightened my leg, or at least tried to, but the pain shot from my left butt cheek all the way to my foot. I felt bile rise in my throat and I was almost sick inside my helmet. I lay back for a moment – then I tried to sit up again. I was shivering. I was holding my leg and trembling like a child. I looked around but nothing seemed to come into focus at all. I was just aware I was on the deck and the bike was in bits that seemed to scatter themselves across the road.

Vaguely, from somewhere in the distance, I heard the sound of a car coming to a stop and then a lady came rushing over. I didn't know who she was but she had an expression of horror on her face, and I worked out that she was the driver of the Mercedes. I think she must've asked if I was alright, I say think because I don't speak Portuguese and I didn't say anything at first. I was just staring at her. I was staring at my leg and I was staring at the bombsite I was sitting in.

'I'm OK.' I found my voice finally and then it was as if I couldn't stop talking. 'I'm fine. I'll be alright, no need to worry, the bike's a bit of a mess, but I'm alright. I'm fine.'

As if to demonstrate that everything was alright, or maybe to convince myself, I tried to get up…but that wasn't happening, and I slumped back down with the pain shooting into my hip. My voice deserted me. I was deep in shock and somehow I seemed to be aware of the fact. I knew I couldn't get up and I looked down to find out why. It took a moment to register that there was something wrong with my leg. I couldn't place what it was at first, but when I tried to move it only the top half obeyed. I could sense no connection between my ankle and my knee and a wave of nausea swept me. *Shit!* I thought. *My left foot is facing the wrong way.* I started to speak but found myself unable to get the words out. I was stuttering, stammering, and I haven't done that since I was a kid.

I never used to stutter; it was something that crept up on me. The first few years of my life in Ireland were idyllic but that all came to an end when I tried to read. Books, words, I couldn't make head nor tail of them. The innate confidence I'd been born with was smashed and there was nothing I could do to stop it. 'Smashed' is my dad's word. He told me he witnessed a self-assured young boy disappear into a cocoon of stuttering silence. Trying to get my head around words that seemed to swim on the page brought my normal measured speech to a halt – and the stammer grew up in its place.

My mum and dad picked up on it early, but it wasn't until we were renting a house in Brentwood, California, that they were able to pin a label on it. Aware I had a serious problem, Dad took me to a reading specialist in Los Angeles where they diagnosed dyslexia. It wasn't something anyone had really heard of in Britain or Ireland at the time, but I'd had the issues since I first picked up a book. The specialist told Dad that the only way to deal with it was time and patience and one-to-one attention. Dad knew that wasn't going to happen in any school, so he undertook the task himself.

Besides being a director and producer, my father John Boorman is a very fine writer as well. He's penned two autobiographies and a novel, as well as most of the scripts for the movies he's made. He knew how vital not only reading was but also real understanding of language, so he spent months and months trying to teach me. It was painstaking work and he was incredibly patient. He'd sit me down for hours at a time and teach me how to spell a simple word – like 'that' for example. I'd be fine while we practiced but then we'd move on to another word and as soon as he tried to recap, I'd be right back where I'd been. I had no recollection of the word at all. It was frustrating, embarrassing, and my feeble attempts to get the spellings out accentuated my stutter even more. It affected every area of my life until I wasn't the same child anymore. Speaking was so difficult that I barely bothered. Seeing me struggle to the point where I withdrew like that just about broke my parents' hearts.

There were lighter moments along with the problems, of course. I remember one sultry day in Ireland when we were all gathered down by the river. The Avonmore runs through our property in County Wicklow and in places it's deep enough to swim. We all swam – it's something we all just wanted to do. The river is this stunning colour, almost like peat, but it's freezing even in the summer. When you're a kid, none of that matters. Dad built a diving board from a wooden plank and, cold or not, we were in the water just about every day. Both my sisters Telsche and Katrine were good swimmers and that day, Katrine was standing on the bank all ready to plunge in when I tried to get her attention.

I could see something was wrong with the picture of her and the water, and I tried to make myself understood.

'Ka…Ka…' I started to say.

'What is it, Charley?' She was ready to perfect the dive.

'Ka-Ka-…'

'What is it, Charley?'

'Ka-Ka-t-r-ine, y-y-you…'

'Oh for God's sake.' With a shake of her head she was already in the water.

'Y-y-you've got your watch on, Katrine,' I said.

Dad brought up that moment with me when we spoke on the phone the other day. I'd called to ask him about my childhood and he was just back from swimming in the river. He's 83 now and not as steady on his feet as he used to be, and I told him he needed to be careful.

'Why?' he said. 'In case I get in trouble and the current sweeps me away? Not a bad way to bow out, Charley; not a bad way to go.'

Half-lying, half-sitting amid the ruins of the motorbike, I was trying to calm the sense of panic that welled up inside. I looked from my twisted leg to the face of another lady and it took a moment before I realised she wasn't the woman who'd clipped me but another woman, a passer-by. There was something comforting about her and she spoke to me in perfect English. She told me her name was Ana and asked what my name was.

'Charley,' I managed. 'My name's Charley. What's wrong with my leg? Why is it facing the wrong way?'

She told me not to worry. She told me everything would be OK. 'I was on my way to work,' she said. 'I stopped because I thought I saw a bag of rubbish flying through the air but then I saw there'd been an accident and it wasn't a bag – it was you.'

I didn't know what to say. My mouth was dry. I could taste vomit on my tongue. I just sat there with both hands trying to control the agony that bled from my thigh. She did her best to calm me. She told me she'd done some nursing with the Red Cross and would take care of me until the ambulance arrived.

'Charley,' she said. 'Everything is going to be OK.'

'I'm fine,' I told her. 'Really, it's alright. I'm OK.'

It was far from alright and I was not OK. I could tell by the way my foot was facing that my leg was badly broken, but the real pain was at the top of my thigh. I thought I'd broken my hip as well as my leg and that scared the shit out of me. A broken hip is life-threatening because it's a cradle for so many vital organs, but it wasn't the fear that bothered me so much as the pain in my buttock and thigh. I could not move from the positon I was in. I had to have both hands under my thigh to support it and keep my knee bent – if I let the leg lie flat my shin would fold back on itself.

It was a mess. A moment before I'd been full of the bike and this new role with Triumph, the upcoming Australia tour that now through the mist of shock seemed to be very far away. Every moment I realised more about my injuries; I grasped that the pain was not limited to my butt cheek or hip and knee, but also in my hand where I was trying to support the leg and my right ankle too. I tried not to move. I tried to sit very still. That was no good. I had to do something or I'd pass out.

'Can you help me?' I said to Ana. I was struggling to keep the tremor from my voice. 'Ana, I can't hold onto my leg like this anymore, there's something wrong with my hand. Can you help me keep the knee up to stop my shin just falling away?'

'Of course.' There was something about her voice that was hopeful, confident: a timbre that was both calm and reassuring. She was kneeling down next to me and I asked if she could wedge her thighs under my right leg and indicated where my fingers gripped just above my knee.

'I need to rest the weight,' I told her. 'I can't hold it up anymore; my hands are shaking too much and I've hurt the right one, I can feel bones moving.' It was a sensation I recognised; I'd had it before when I smashed my hands racing the Dakar Rally.

Very gently, Ana worked her knees under my thigh and that took the pain from my hands and eased it a little in my leg. We sat like that as the muscles in my groin gradually began to relax, and I felt some relief. I couldn't move. Ana couldn't move. That was the only position that kept the pain in some kind of check and that's how we were when I heard the wail of sirens and moments later I saw the ambulance arrive.

By this time most of the guys from Triumph were there; they had been a little way behind me when we left the hotel and had seen the carnage ahead. It was the last thing they'd expected, of course, and they were looking pretty panicked. I picked up on that and my own fears redoubled. Moments before it had just been me and Ana and now there were people everywhere. The police arrived to cordon off the area and keep traffic moving, then the paramedics started to deal with my leg. Ana was on her knees in the gravel still supporting me with her thighs and I'd given no thought to how uncomfortable that had to be. She made no complaint. She was only concerned about me. By the time they finally stretchered me away her knees were skinned to the point they bled.

I don't know how much time had passed. When something like this goes down time has a way of standing still. I had no idea how much damage had been done to my left leg, but I knew it wasn't good and all sorts of thoughts were hammering away in my head. I didn't know it then but my right ankle was dislocated as well as broken, and it hurt like hell. Ever the optimist, I thought perhaps I'd bashed it on the kerbstone and it was just badly bruised. I remember the guys from Triumph looking really perturbed, but thought that might've been because I was sitting on what was left of a disintegrated Tiger.

With the paramedics taking charge Ana could finally get her thighs out from under my legs. She disappeared from my field of vision and that disturbed me because she had quickly become my only source of solace. I was on my back with my helmet still on as the paramedics stabilised my neck. They wanted to take my helmet off and they clearly weren't aware that new helmets have these little red cords attached. When they're pulled, they disengage the cheek portion which makes removing the rest of it easy. At that point their fumbling with it was working my neck over pretty good despite the brace, so I told them I'd do it. They weren't up for that though; they didn't want me lifting my arms. I tried to explain what they had to do and between us we finally managed to get my helmet off.

I think that was the moment when things began to go pear-shaped. The paramedics produced a pair of scissors and started to cut at my boots. That wasn't going to happen. I loved those boots, brand new from Rev-It, so I told them they could take them off – there was no need to cut them away. It's weird the kind of details that bother you in times like that. There I was with pain soaking the entire lower half of my body and all I could think about was how much I loved those boots. It didn't end there though; as soon as my boots were off they set about cutting the jacket and I had to stop them again.

'You're not doing that,' I said. 'There's no need. I can move my arms. There's no need to cut the jacket off.'

They let the jacket be and a few minutes later a doctor arrived in a car and took charge of the situation. With my boots gone the paramedics took their scissors to my trouser leg and cut all the way up. I couldn't see much because I was no longer sitting up. With my neck in a brace I was lying on my back and they wouldn't let me lift my head. Suddenly everything stopped. I could feel a real chill in the air as a discussion broke out in Portuguese that was quiet and sombre. The atmosphere had definitely changed.

Like a damp cloth, that chill rippled through me again. A creeping sensation that seemed to slow the blood in my veins. I still didn't know what they'd found but clearly there was something very wrong. Then I noticed the blood. There was blood on the ground and I'd spotted blood on Ana's jacket while she was supporting me as well. For some reason, I hadn't associated that blood with me. I did now though, and blood wasn't good. Blood wasn't good at all.

Before I could find out what was going on I felt a hand on my leg then something jabbed all the way into my groin. I almost shrieked from the pain. Sweat on my brow, I felt as if I was going to throw up. I felt down with my hand and found some kind of stick or pole poking me in the groin. *What the fuck?* I thought, then realised they were fitting something to my leg. It took a moment or two before I worked out it was a splint. The next thing I knew the pain was so intense I was yelling at them, telling them to stop whatever it was they were doing. They didn't, and the pain raced all the way up my body into my head. With the splint in place, the doctor was attempting to straighten my leg.

I was bleeding. I could see a whole lot of blood on the pavement now and that sent shockwaves through me yet again. I began to slip inside myself, that's the only way I can describe it – this bubble of consciousness where I'm on my own and all that's happening is going on outside that bubble and it's distant and muffled, seeming very far away, and nothing to do with me.

But it was to do with me. This was all to do with me. I could feel a hand on my right leg – someone was rubbing, massaging, working the muscles under the skin. One of the paramedics put his face close to mine, entering my bubble for a moment, and I heard him tell me that my right ankle was broken as well. Trying to take that in, I looked around and saw the guys from Triumph directing traffic. Nigel Land from marketing remained with me, together with one of his colleagues, Mark. He was holding my hand as I lay there with the paramedics working on my leg. I can still remember the warmth of that human touch; after Ana had gone I gripped his hand until they loaded me into the ambulance. I'm so grateful for that, for those two guys and all the others; the level of concern they showed was so typical of the way things have been ever since we started working together. Nigel was by my side from the moment he came upon the accident until they wheeled me out of theatre later that night.

Right now, though, I was nowhere near theatre; I was at the side of the road and still inside my protective bubble. It wasn't the first time I'd been in a bubble; the last time was in the south of France with Neil Crabtree-Taylor, a friend I've known for years. We were in a Renault 5 and Neil was driving. I was in the passenger seat and Olivia in the back. As we came around a corner this white Lada four-wheel-drive drifted to our side of the road, the driver six times over the legal alcohol limit. He hit us head on: a combined speed of 100mph. Olly dislocated her shoulder, multiple fractures down her arm, and Neil shattered his knee. I went through the windscreen. It all happened so fast I knew nothing about it at all.

When she started to come round from the shock, Olly could see me lying with my head on the dashboard and blood pouring from my face. There was so much blood that the old-style pen holders in the dash were full to brimming. For a moment, she thought I was dead. Then I suddenly sat up, looked around at the carnage and threw open the passenger door. I told Olly and Neil they had to get out because we didn't know if the car was going to catch on fire. I had no idea how bad my face was until I looked in the wing-mirror and saw the skin literally hanging off. From beneath my eye to the base of my jaw, it was as if someone had peeled it back – and eight months later I would still be picking bits of glass from my scalp. As we waited for an ambulance to show I up I remember that protective bubble where there was no one in the world save Olly, Neil and me.

That bubble had burst when we got to the hospital, and by the side of the road in Portugal I could feel it begin to go again. I didn't think the worst yet; I was too busy trying to deal with the pain. Now that my left leg was in a splint the paramedics manoeuvred me onto a solid stretcher and the pain was just incredible. Cold, hard plastic all around me, the base digging into my hip. I almost passed out then I saw the look on the doctor's face and was shaken from the stupor again.

'Olly,' I said, spotting Nigel standing next to the doctor with his helmet under his arm. 'Nigel, call my wife, Olivia... tell her what happened, will you? Give her a call.'

'It's alright,' he said. 'We're on it, Charley. I just spoke to Billy on the phone.'

Billy Ward, my friend and sometime manager; if Nigel had spoken to him then Billy would be speaking to Olly. She would know what had happened. She'd be on her way. That thought gave me a little comfort.

By now I was in the back of the ambulance on that ghastly gurney and the pain in my hip had worsened still. I could not move; my right leg incapacitated and my left in a splint, again I sought the doctor. 'How bad is this?' I said. 'Is everything OK with my legs?'

For a long moment, he looked at me – and then he shook his head. 'The break is bad, very bad. The bones have punctured the skin.'

'What?' I gawped, mouth hanging open. 'Whose skin? What skin? What do you mean the bones have punctured the skin?'

'The tibia and fibula, they're sticking out of your leg. We have to be very careful now or infection will set in.'

LIGHTS AND SIRENS

That wasn't the first time I came off a motorbike; far from it. Back when I was a kid in Ireland I fell off a monkey bike not long after my dad discovered how badly dyslexic I was. I say fell off it – actually he saved me before it crashed into a barbed-wire fence.

It was around the time he made a film called *Zardoz*, which he shot close to where we lived. I must've been six or seven, and that's when I met Jason Connery for the first time. Jason's dad, Sean, was starring in the movie, and the family were staying at our house while the movie was made. Our dads had work to do; Jason and I, however, were messing about on the monkey bike.

The house was an old vicarage Dad bought in 1969 during an out-of-body experience while we were on holiday in Ireland. He had sold his place in Putney for £10,000 and wasn't sure where he wanted to live. Another house in London was an option, as was LA, but as he drove around County Wicklow he came across an auction at an estate agent's office and stopped.

I was only three, but the way Dad tells it, something surreal happened. As he stood at the back of the crowd, watching the bidding, he seemed to escape his body and floated up to the ceiling from where he watched for a while before slipping back into his body again. Only then did he realise that one of the bidders was him. He'd bought the property without knowing that was his intention when he walked in. He's been in Ireland ever since.

It turned out to be the best thing he ever did. As far as his children were concerned it was fabulous; a large old house and grounds that included meadow and pasture, with a river running through it. We grew up there when the tensions with the Irish Republicans were at their height. Dad tells a story about one night when he saw a set of headlights on the drive as someone approached from the road. A car pulled up and two men dressed in dark-coloured clothing got out and came up to the house. Dad was pretty sure who they were, if not why they were there. IRA men; they wanted to use the land he'd bought to t rain their young men. Back in those days the IRA was split into two different factions: the Provisionals and the Official IRA who were known as the 'Stickies'. It was these guys who came to the house. Dad wasn't up for anyone being on his land and he's not known for being a shrinking violet. He told them he wasn't happy about it and, to his amazement, they said they wouldn't impose anything on him – he had to agree to it. He explained that he had four young children and didn't think it was a good idea at all. It took a few minutes of silence, some dark looks shooting back and forth…then the Stickies left. We never saw them again.

I count myself very lucky because it was a wonderful place to be a kid. My dad's parents were publicans and my mum grew up on a farm in northern Germany, so they were both from pretty normal stock. There were no airs or graces, no delusions of grandeur; it was all very homely and down-to-earth. Mum used to have a jug of pancake mix ready all the time in case anyone should show up hungry. We had a cleaner and a couple of other people to help out around the place, but we all sat down to meals together.

We lived in Annamoe, an idyllic spot deep in the country surrounded by lanes and hills, ancient forests and lakes. I used to disappear for hours on end, walking, swimming, riding my sister's horse bareback, and listening out for the rasping rattle of dirt bikes. Long before I was old enough to ride one myself, I'd listen to local lads trekking off-road and was captivated. I used to get so lost in my surroundings that the only thing that could bring me back was Mum standing outside the kitchen door with a megaphone, calling us in for lunch or dinner.

Anyway, back to that day in the 1970s, with the filming of *Zardoz*. Having a movie filmed close to where we lived was nothing new; it was no different to being on location, just that the location was County Wicklow. I'd already been with Dad during the filming of *Deliverance*: indeed, I had a small role (no, I wasn't the banjo player) as Jon Voight's son. As I said before, Dad took us with him whenever he could and made use of us whenever children were called for in a particular scene. Why pay a child actor when he already had four of his own? We were always up for it – I mean, who wouldn't be? It was just like playing a game, only there was this guy on the other side of a camera filming it, and we paid no attention to him. I had no real idea what it actually meant. In fact, I don't believe I really grasped the impact my father had on the movie world until *Excalibur* was shown at Cannes.

This time around, with the Connerys staying at the house during filming, I had a lot of time to spend with Jason. I guess he would've been about ten, and dossing around with him for days on end was my first real memory of being on a motorbike. When people think of me and biking mates they tend to think of Ewan McGregor. It's true he and I have undertaken some pretty epic rides together, but Jason's been a big part of my biking life as well.

That day we were trying to get this little monkey bike going. Monkeys are miniature motorcycles; the first came out in 1961 and they called it the Z100. It had 4.5 horsepower with a seat that was only 22 inches off the ground, a four-stroke engine and no suspension. The suspension changed over the years with springs added at the front initially, but by 1974 they were on the back as well.

I remember it seemed to take forever to get the thing started. Once we managed it, we took turns blatting across my dad's lawn while our fathers knocked a tennis ball about as they discussed what was going on with the movie. Suddenly, on what was about to be my last ride of the day, I found myself pretty much out of control and making straight for a barbed wire fence. Whether by chance or design, somehow my dad was standing right there. As I came screaming past he reached down as nonchalant as you like, grabbed a handful of flowing locks and lifted me clear. I swung like a rag doll as the bike continued its trajectory and crashed into the barbed wire fence.

I'd been unhurt then save for my wounded pride, but now, lying on that plastic gurney in Portugal, shattered bones sticking out of my skin, I knew things were very different. I could see in my mind's eye the blood on the ground, the blood on Ana's jacket. Now I knew the blood was mine and it had spilled from my wounded leg. I felt very cold, and yet a film of sweat coated my skin. One of the paramedics said something about the hospital, and I made sure I took it in. Even in shock I knew I needed to be aware of where they were taking me. The guy said something else I didn't understand and I made him tell me again. The Centro Hospitalar in Portimão. I recognised that part because Portimão is where they hold the Portuguese round of World Superbikes.

I don't remember much about the journey apart from the sirens ringing in my head. The back doors of the ambulance opened and I was lifted out, then wheeled straight to intensive care. I wanted Olivia, I wanted to see my wife but she was miles away in London. I was desperate to phone her, talk to her. I wanted to hear her voice but right now the nurses set about tending my wounds and I couldn't reach my phone; I didn't even know where it was.

I was still lying on that solid sheet of plastic and I cannot describe how it felt. There was something about the position that was just awful, and I could think of nothing but the pain in my leg. Five hours later I was still thinking about it because I was still on that fucking gurney. By then I'd been scanned and X-rayed and my wounds irrigated with antiseptic solution again and again. The pain got so bad I was begging them to find me some padding or move me to a mattress or something because I couldn't take any more. No matter how I tried to shift my position the pain was always there.

All my begging was to no avail. Nothing happened. They didn't move me. They kept me strapped to that gurney, and I could've cried. My mouth was so dry I could barely peel my tongue from where it stuck to the roof. My lips were cracked. I was as thirsty as I think I've ever been. I wasn't allowed any water as they had me booked for theatre and I couldn't take any fluids. The nurses were sympathetic though; seeing how bad my lips were, one of them brought a cup of water and a small sponge that she dipped and pressed to my mouth.

My outer garments were gone but I was still wearing the down-filled puffa I'd put on underneath to keep warm. Before anyone realised what the implications would be, someone took up a pair of scissors; suddenly the room was a cloud of feathers. Millions of fragments of duck down were floating all over the intensive care unit, and like some maniacal patient in a bad B-movie I was giggling away like a child.

The surgeon came to see me, a man called Souza; he told me I needed a number of operations and I needed them now. He spoke good English as most of the nurses seemed to, explaining that my left leg was the most serious and that with the way the bones had been exposed to the road there was a real danger of infection. With so much alien material around by way of dirt and dust, and fragments of clothing, they had to be fastidious in making sure nothing got into the wound. Infection would be critical and he pulled no punches when he told me I could easily lose my leg,

That comment really chilled me. Even with blood on the ground and bones sticking out of me, I hadn't considered the possibility I might lose my leg. The sweat was back, sticking to me like a suffocating second skin. I tried to concentrate as he told me they were going to plate the bone as soon as they could get me into theatre. He described the procedure, though I didn't take it in. He reiterated the need to be scrupulous when it came to irrigation to make sure infection did not set in.

Gone were the giggles at flying feathers. I lay there cold as stone, trying to imagine life without a leg. Even if it was amputated below the knee I knew I could never ride a motorbike. I'd never be able to walk without a crutch or a prosthesis. I'd never be the same again.

It was in the back of my throat, that sickly sensation, and I tried to tell myself it would not come to that. I forced myself to be confident. I forced myself to think about other riders who'd come back from much worse than this. I remembered Barry Sheene returning to racing with more bolts, plates and pins in his legs than anyone had ever seen. Both legs had been shattered at Indianapolis back in the day; the X-rays had been all over the newspapers when I was a kid.

After the doctor left, the nurses worked on irrigating the wound all over again. They were meticulous, leaving nothing to chance, but I'd been lying in exactly the same position for hours and all my muscles had seized. It wasn't just the physical discomfort; the pain gravitated to my mind. Claustrophobia suddenly swamped me. I'd never experienced it before and I felt the panic set in.

It consumed me, working through every sinew of my being like a fever. I could barely see. I couldn't speak. I couldn't breathe without gasping. My brain seemed to have separated itself from the rest of my body, my thoughts and emotions clashing in a riot that felt like another physical pain. I had to deal with this. I had to concentrate. I had to focus on something other than the maelstrom in my head. Each breath was short and stunted. I had to force myself to inhale and exhale again. When my breathing finally began to ease, I sought the silence that's been my failsafe since I was a kid.

I'd learned about silence from the Quakers, but it wasn't something I stuck a label on when I was a kid. Back then when I couldn't get the words out I'd just clam up. I'd slip into a silence where I would sit and watch the world from a corner. If I didn't say anything, I didn't stutter – and people wouldn't lose patience with me. When I was silent everything was OK. I could think instead of speak and when I was thinking the words came easily. I would disappear within myself. Even if I was in a room full of people, in my mind I could always be somewhere else.

I loved the silence of where we lived in Ireland. Annamoe is such a sleepy little place, surrounded by hills that go on for miles and miles. In many areas, there aren't even any telephone poles, it's why so many period movies are made there. For me it was a sanctuary; I'd clear off into the hills on my own, explore the river and woodlands, make my way through the ancient forests and see wildlife I'd never otherwise have seen. I remember when I finally got my first bike I'd fill it with petrol then strap a spare tank on the back and ride the heather-topped hills until the fuel ran out, before refilling the tank and riding back.

I remember the sense of calm. There was something about there being no people around that I was really into. It was such a contrast to the bustle of our house. It wasn't just our family – there were always other people there. My mum loved to cook and she could produce amazing dishes that no one had ever seen. Her father fought for Germany in World War I and was wounded three times. By the time World War II came around he was much older, and didn't want to fight because he'd seen first-hand the carnage and suffering that war brings. He refused to go and the family suffered because of it. During the lean years when food was scarce they had to improvise, and maybe that's where Mum found her culinary imagination.

Dad in particular made use of her talents. When he was looking to raise money for a movie he'd meet with Hollywood producers and financiers, but instead of dining at restaurants or hotels he'd invite them back to the house. Totally informal, it was a home from home and a little chaotic with four children running around. But it was real life and not something these big-time movie men were used to at all. They loved it, the homely feel and personal touch. Dad used to say it was the icing on the cake that sealed the deal.

So there were always people in the house, and looking back some of them were pretty famous – but none of that mattered, it was lost on a boy like me. All I cared about was not having to say too much, and people in the house meant loads of great food and a kitchen that was a hive of activity. I think it's where I learned to love cooking too. I got used to being around lots of people but not really being present at all. That would all change later, but in the early days of my dyslexia it was how I coped with the trauma, and that's how I was coping with the feelings of claustrophobia now.

While I was retreating into my shell in the hospital, my wife was back in London, taking care of the house and making sure our daughters had everything they needed. She'd also been working as a mentor to young offenders who had served their prison time with a charity called Key4Life, which is something I really admire about her. It's indicative of the kind of person she is. There's a real doggedness about Olly; a sense of justice and fair play; a solidity I recognised in her straight away. During those early days when we'd go out on date and then I'd take off without kissing her, I should've been more assertive. Maybe I was mindful of the age gap – but then I was never very good with women in the first place.

Until Olivia got the phone call from Billy she had no idea I'd come off the bike or how serious a condition I was in. Billy is what I guess you could call my manager (though the title can really be shared between him and my agent, Robert Kirby). Just as he'd promised, Nigel had called Billy while I was still lying in agony beside the road. As soon as Billy hung up, he phoned Olly at home.

'Olly,' he said. 'It's Billy here. Have you talked to Charley today?'

'Yes, I spoke to him just now.'

'When just now? How long ago?'

'I don't know, maybe 20 minutes, half an hour or something. He was just leaving the hotel.'

'Ah,' Billy said. 'So you don't know what's happened then.'

He had my wife's attention now. I can just see her shifting the phone from one hand to the other.

'Charley's had an accident,' Billy told her. 'He's come off his bike and might've broken his leg. He's alright though, there's nothing to worry about.'

'Are you sure he's alright? Are you sure it's just a broken leg?'

'He's fine, Olly. The guys from Triumph are taking care of him.'

Fine. Now there's a word to cover a multitude of sins. That's the word I used when I spoke to my eldest daughter Doone after I'd come off the bike in Dakar and broken my hands. I've heard people say they're fine when what they really mean is they're frightened, insecure, nervous and emotional. In this case fine meant six hours in surgery with a shattered tibia and fibula. It meant more broken bones in my hand and a broken (not to mention dislocated) ankle. It meant I might lose my leg and never walk unaided again.

Just as my father's unconventional job and its influence on our family life always seemed completely normal to me, my daughters Doone and Kinvara have lived with mine for as long as they can remember. We've always known the risks of me riding a motorbike – in an instant, something can go down that might change your life forever. The same can be said of a car, but on a bike you're more exposed so the dangers are that much greater. As I was about to learn, the massive advancements in treating leg injuries over the past few years are largely down to the victims of motorcycle accidents. Most people ease up on the riskier side of stuff when they have children, but that doesn't tend to be the case with bikers. Most of the guys racing professionally are married with kids and they risk their lives every time they go out on track. It's no different with me – my whole life has been about motorbikes and I've had some hairy moments – but the funny thing is, often it's the thought of the children that has kept me going. We've always been a 'can do' family and neither of the girls, nor my wife, have ever questioned the life I've chosen. If anything the reverse has been true; not only have they never taken issue with anything I've done no matter how dangerous, but they've backed and encouraged me every step of the way. I think a long time ago they realised that this is pretty much the only way I can make a living.

As I lay there in hospital Olivia had no idea how bad the accident was. All she'd been told was that I'd broken my leg – and that was no big deal, she'd seen plenty of broken limbs before, like Ewan's the day before we were due to go skiing a month or so before *Long Way Down*.

Olly's a pragmatist; little fazes her, and when something goes wrong emotions don't come into it. She focuses on what needs to be done. That's probably just as well given the life she's had being married to me. A broken leg wasn't anything to get overly emotional about – it just meant an Aircast boot or a bit of plaster, some discomfort and itching, a little muscle wastage maybe – nothing to be particularly concerned with.

With that in mind she decided she wouldn't do anything until she had more information. She was aware that Nigel had phoned Billy from the scene of the accident so I'd probably be on my way to hospital. Billy told her that someone would phone with an update later and she would probably have to fly down to bring me home.

The first available flight wasn't until early the following morning, but that was alright because there was the dog to think about. Someone would need to look after Ziggy, our springer spaniel – who's still relatively spring-like but almost deaf at 14. Olly set about making preparations until a little later Nigel called from the hospital to tell her I'd gone into surgery, and explained that I needed several operations.

As soon as she heard that, Olly realised it wasn't quite as simple as a broken leg after all. She immediately booked a flight out to Faro from Gatwick, then called back to tell Nigel she would arrive the following morning. He told her he'd pick her up, and in the meantime he wasn't going to leave the hospital until I was out of theatre and in the recovery room. He was conscious of how upset I'd been – and that I was 1,500 miles from home.

Nigel was amazing and I'm so grateful to him. He didn't leave my side that day apart from when I was in surgery, and it was after 10pm when I was finally moved to a ward. All I kept saying was how sorry I was and how I'd let everyone down, and he told me not to be so silly. He said he'd spoken to my wife and she had a flight booked for 6.30 in the morning. He would meet her and make sure she had somewhere to stay. I was pretty emotional by then, full of anaesthetic and anxiety. I found myself apologising for screwing things up all over again.

'Forget about it,' he said. 'It happens, Charley; riding a bike it's part of the game.' Pretty knackered himself by then, he told me to get some rest and he'd bring Olly to see me first thing.

Still incoherent from the anaesthetic, I woke in the recovery room not knowing where I was. In a rush it all came back to me – and as I looked down at my legs, for a moment I couldn't tell if they were both there. Panic seized me and I managed to take my weight on one elbow to get a better look. The nurse was on her feet and it took a moment before I was sure I still had both of mine.

It was with some relief that I lay back as they wheeled me to a ward before transferring me to a bed. It was dark outside and the room only dimly lit. All manner of thoughts seemed to plague me; not least what the doctor had said about infection and losing my leg. Those thoughts seemed to evaporate, however, as I caught a sound I couldn't quite identify – a sort of grunting almost like a pig. The nurses left me to get some sleep and I lay there wondering why they'd put me in a room with a pig. Half awake and half dreaming, I was trying to figure out what the fuck they were doing with a pig in the hospital.

Then I picked up another sound. It was loud and it was brief and it didn't come alone. A smell accompanied it, something so bad I started to gag. I knew what it was but still it took another few seconds before I realised it wasn't a pig I could hear; the grunting sound was the snore of another patient in his own peaceful if deafening oblivion.

Looking across the room I could just about make him out: bald-headed and bearded with one arm in a sling. His name was Ragnar (or at least that's what we're going to call him for the purposes of this narrative). No names, no pack drill, just a traveller from Denmark, the oldest swinger in town, his shoulder swollen and purple with bruising.

When I woke up in the morning he was looking at my bandaged legs with a puzzled expression on his face.

'Morning,' he said in English. 'My name's Ragnar. From Denmark. What happened to you?'

'Motorbike accident,' I told him. 'I'm Charley. I ride motorbikes. Or at least I did.'

Slowly he nodded. 'I know you. I think I've seen you somewhere...maybe on TV?'

'I rode around the world,' I told him. 'A few years back, I rode a motorbike around the world. *Long Way Round*, that's what we called the show.'

'Ah,' he said. 'So that's where I've seen you. I knew your face was familiar. How're you feeling? Hungry? They'll be bringing breakfast in a bit.'

I tried to sit up, but it wasn't easy with only one working hand. 'So what happened to you?' I asked him. 'Why're you here?'

One bushy eyebrow arched, and he glanced down at his shoulder. 'I was in the bar. No, that's not right – I was on the bar. I was crawling.'

'Crawling on the bar? Are you kidding?'

'No, I can remember that part quite clearly.' He looked a little thoughtful. 'I'd had a couple of drinks and was crawling on the bar. I don't remember too much after that... but my shoulder's broken, so I suppose I must've fallen off.'

Looking back, I'm incredibly grateful to my dad for spending so much time with me when it was obvious I was having trouble learning to read. We've talked about it a lot and he remembers me as having what he called an 'easy and assured sense of humour'. The only boy among three girls, I was the baby brother who seemed to get away with everything. One day after supper when I was about four, I was sitting in a chair sucking my thumb. My sisters were washing up and Katrine looked round, shaking her head. 'How come Charley doesn't ever do anything?' she said. 'He never lifts a finger.'

My gaze fixed on hers. Without taking my thumb from my mouth, I raised a nonchalant pinky.

So when I lost my confidence and gained the stammer that marked the rest of my childhood, Dad spoke to lots of different speech therapists, both here and in America. He discovered that there's a reaction in the brain that occurs when anyone sets about trying to learn a new skill. Something kicks into gear and the brain opens up the short-term memory. After that, another section opens the medium-term, and finally the long-term banks come into play until the skill is stored as a reference point. For some reason, with people like me the memory banks refuse to open. They have to be teased into action and that takes time, effort and constant revisiting. The result is what appears to others to be forgetfulness, and that's been the bane of my life ever since.

There are millions of such sufferers all over the world and these days I try to highlight the condition as much as I can. A couple of years ago I was on a bike tour in Australia with a party of guests when a woman approached me. She'd found out I was in the country and looked up what hotel I would be in on a particular night, then driven ten hours with her dyslexic son just so he could talk to me. I spent hours with that guy, sitting on a log in the desert talking about how he couldn't get his head around words, and how he had the same problem with memory that I did.

He too had a stutter and I told him I got over mine in the same way as King George. If you've seen the film *The King's Speech* you'll know what I'm talking about. I was taught to sing what I wanted to say and when I was singing I wouldn't stutter. I kept that up day after day until gradually the stammering eased. It's not completely gone – if I get really stressed it creeps in and I can't get my tongue around what I'm trying to say. It's all about confidence, and confidence is a delicate thing.

Right now, mine had been ripped away by a totally avoidable accident. Waking up in a two-bed ward with Ragnar that first morning, I checked my left leg and it didn't look so bad. It was dressed with a regular crepe-style bandage; my foot wasn't too swollen.

While we were waiting for the hospital caterers to bring us breakfast I asked Ragnar what he was doing in Portugal. He told me that he'd lost his wife a few years ago and was there on his own. He explained that during a long and happy marriage the two of them had taken regular road trips in a motorhome to avoid the Scandinavian winter. A seasoned traveller still, after his wife died Ragnar carried on with the business of wintering in warmer climes. He'd drive across Europe to the Algarve where you can park your motorhome at campsites for next to nothing, and see out the cold weather. 'Besides,' he added. 'Where else can you get a beer for 90 cents?'

I wasn't really up for too much chat that morning; my mind was on my leg. I remember the word 'shattered' being used by the surgeon. A shattered left tibia and fibula where fragments of bone had exploded through a wound in the skin. In the back of my mind the word 'infection' loomed like some dark and malevolent shadow. When the surgeon made his rounds he checked the dressing and explained to me what he'd done. He'd pinned the leg with a screw placed horizontally below the knee, and fixed a plate on the remains of the tibia. It seemed pretty standard stuff and I told myself I was on the mend. All I had to do now was get home and get on.

Unfortunately, though I couldn't have known it at the time, that sense of confidence was greatly misplaced. I'd find that out when I finally got back to London. For now though, my right ankle was broken, had also been pinned, and was very swollen. There were pins in my right hand at the junction between my thumb and index finger, and it was also heavily bandaged. It was a bit of a clusterfuck, I thought – my first event with Triumph and there I was lying in a hospital bed. At least Olly was on her way, and I was longing to see her.

I realised I was ravenously hungry, with nothing in my stomach since breakfast at the hotel the previous morning. Finally, the caterer arrived with a roll, some juice and a couple of slivers of cheese. An older woman, she placed the tray on a little wheeled table – which would've been fine if I'd been able to reach it. But the only part of my body I could move was my left hand, and the table was over by the window. She did not seem to notice, placing the tray down and heading immediately for the door. Ragnar was more mobile than I was, though he was still bandaged and hampered with his dislocated shoulder. Sitting up, he managed to get the woman's attention and indicated that she needed to talk to me. My Portuguese is non-existent and she didn't speak much English, but with smiles and gestures, a combination of sad eyes and sign language, I managed to get her to understand that I needed the table wheeled over to my bed.

As it turned out I would be in that hospital for a week and the dance with food and tables would repeat every mealtime. As the time came for the caterers to show up, Ragnar and I would check the location of the tables and take bets on where the food would be put and where the tables would end up. It was the same every time; not once were those pesky tables wheeled where they needed to be.

Don't get me wrong, I'm not complaining – it was just a part of the daily ritual, and incapacitated as we were it was something of a distraction. Overall the Portuguese staff were exceptional. Their attention to detail, particularly regarding the prevention of any infection, was spectacular. So much can go wrong when a bone breaks through the skin. With armoured jeans or any other kind of clothing the tiniest fragments can get inside the wound and cause all sorts of problems. They were meticulous both at the roadside and after they had brought me in. Every day from that point on they made sure everything was cleaned, cleaned and cleaned again.

Still, there's nothing quite like immobility for the demons to creep in – even after a few hours. I've been active all my life, spending seven or eight months a year on the road, and there I was laid up in bed with God knows how many months of rehabilitation ahead. I was gutted, kicking myself for coming off the bike when there had been nothing but clear blue skies ahead. But that was yesterday. Today a whole bank of clouds was looming in my mind and I had to be careful not to slump into depression.

I still had to make a living and in just a few weeks I was supposed to be on another 'Ride with Charley Boorman' motorbike tour in Australia. People pay good money to be on those expeditions and, as you might imagine, they expect to see me. We started out in South Africa a few years back then extended into Australia. Later this year we'd be launching our first expedition to South America – but before that I was supposed to be making an attempt on the Darien Gap.

The Gap is an infamous stretch of jungle in South America; we had a TV show booked with Channel 5 where we planned to make the crossing on motorbikes. That was never going to be easy – it's hard enough on four wheels and a potential nightmare on two. It's almost 100 miles of treacherous terrain where the Pan-American Highway is broken between the Darien Province of northern Panama and the Choco Department in Colombia, and one of the most difficult-to-negotiate passages of land anywhere in the world. It was something Russ Malkin and I first talked about when I was racing the Dakar ten years previously, and I'd revisited the idea more recently during the excursions I've made in Canada, South Africa and the USA. Almost 100 miles of swamp and rainforest, rife with bandits and drug dealers – there was no way I would be able to do it now. I knew I had to get hold of Russ and see if the TV company would delay the proposal. I promised myself I would still do it though, and decided that an attempt on the Gap was the target for my full recovery.

I was desperate now to see Olly. When you're far from home, in pain and unsure of what's going to happen, a familiar, loving face is all you want. To that end I had a lot of sympathy for Ragnar; over the next week I'd have Olivia with me and the lads from Triumph popping in and out. The only person Ragnar had to visit him was a born-again Christian he barely knew. I met him that first day; he was a personable enough guy, well-meaning of course, but with an agenda. When he saw me he couldn't believe it. He told me he knew who I was because I'd already met his kids. I have to say I didn't recall the meeting – apparently it had been a brief encounter on the road somewhere during one of my expeditions. But I could tell he saw it as a sign and his focus switched from Ragnar to me.

He was pretty enthusiastic. He had a book he wanted to pass on but I told him I didn't find reading easy because of my dyslexia. I'm not religious in any conventional sense, though that doesn't mean I don't think about things; I'm spiritual in my own way. The sojourns I used to take alone in the Wicklow Mountains when I was a kid, the forests, the rivers; if anything, it's the natural world and the natural order of things that I have an affinity with.

The guy didn't look as though he was going to quit that easily, but fortunately Nigel came in to let me know Olly had made the first flight out from Gatwick. He was going to pick her up from the airport and take her to a hotel close to the hospital. That way she'd be able to walk over to see me rather than have to hire a vehicle.

'By the way,' he said. 'We found the missing wheel.'

'What missing wheel?' I asked him.

'Charley, the bike was in bits. If it had been fitted with a self-destruct button you couldn't have done more damage. The driveshaft was under your leg and the front wheel was a hundred yards down that side road in somebody's garden.'

'There was blood on the wall,' I said. Either I remembered or someone had told me. 'I must've hit the wall. The car wasn't damaged. I must've hit the wall when I peeled off trying to avoid the car.'

'Probably,' Nigel said. 'Anyway, you're here and alive.'

I peered down the length of the bed. 'Three of four limbs out of commission...no, I guess it's not as bad as we thought.'

He took off then and came back with Olly and my relief at seeing her wasn't only limited to the warm rush of joyous emotion. There were other pressing issues – and I'm not speaking metaphorically. I needed to take a shit, which meant a bedpan and somebody wiping up – and that wasn't going to be a nurse or hospital orderly. I don't know how many of you have experienced hospital bedpans; they come in all shapes, sizes and a variety of colours, and I suppose the only thing they've got going for them is the fact that they're no longer made of metal.

There's nothing more uncomfortable or ignominious than trying to wrestle one under your arse when you're laid up in bed with three of your limbs out of order. Add the fact that you're not alone in the room, and also that a bedpan is dry. See where this is going? There's the smell to contend with, which can be bad enough in the loo where there's water and a flush – but it's on a different level when you're talking about laying logs (or rabbit pellets in my case) on a dry surface. That's assuming you get to make the deposit in the first place. Anaesthetic – and I've had a few – has this way of stopping up the tubes like nothing else. It takes all the effort a wounded man can muster to squeeze out a couple of nuggets. No, I needed someone I knew, someone who loved me, to clean up after I was done.

(Talking of bedpans: it wasn't just taking a shit that was an issue. All the time I was in the ward I had a catheter. Easy-Pee, I called it; you just lie there and go without even being aware you're passing water. The only problem is taking it out. In my case it was early in the morning, so early it was still dark. A nurse came in and started talking at me. At the same time, she reached under the blankets, grabbed the tube and pulled it out. It was horrendous. Not so much from the pain – which was bad enough – but more from the shock.)

Anyway, bodily functions aside – my wife was there, and once I'd been relieved, we could get on with the business of trying to get home. One thing I'd say right here is that travel insurance is absolutely vital. It needs to be comprehensive. Even if you're in Europe you should never leave home without it. I don't. No matter where I'm going or who with, I leave nothing to chance and nothing to anybody else.

We got stuck into the details, or rather Olly did. The lack of WiFi in the hospital meant that most of the work had to be done from her hotel bedroom. She contacted the travel insurance company and then my private health insurance, which I keep up to date because of how much of the year I'm away. Everything seemed to be OK. It actually appeared quite straightforward, back in the beginning. The air ambulance to take us back to London was provisionally booked for the following Tuesday. That would be a week to the day after the accident. It was a while to wait, but I'd lost blood and my red cell count was lower than the 10 it had to be in order to be able to fly.

She was in and out all day, bringing food and news of what was going on. She'd spoken to the King Edward VII private hospital in London after discussing the situation with my sister Katrine. Katrine is older than Daisy and I, the second of the four children. She's very sociable and knows an awful lot of people, making her very good in a crisis; this wouldn't be the first time we'd turned to her for assistance.

Katrine acted in Paris for more than ten years and more recently her first feature film *Me and Me Dad* was an official selection at Cannes. She and her husband, artist and novelist Danny Moynihan, have been together for 22 years and have two children called Kit and Tallulah. When I was at school in Banbury during my teens Katrine lived in London, and whenever Daisy and I had long weekend breaks we'd stay with her if Mum and Dad were away. In those days she was pretty crazy and the house was manic with visitors. I remember Katrine dressing in these mad outfits with lots of avant-garde people around; actors, painters, musicians. Daisy and I would sit in the corner of her living room watching the mayhem and creative madness.

It was actually through Katrine that I became really close to Jason. He was more her friend than mine to begin with, which makes sense as he's a little older than I am. It was a time when my sister took me under her wing. She would choose clothes for me and take me shopping. In the fifth form at school we could wear our own clothes instead of a uniform so long as it was jacket and tie. I remember she bought me a dicky bow once, but I never had the balls to wear it.

So Olly had spoken to Katrine, confident and brilliant in a crisis – and though we didn't know it, we were about to hit a crisis. One of Katrine's great friends is a heart surgeon called Jullien Gaer, and it was he who suggested I go to King Edward VII to see an orthopaedic consultant he rated by the name of Curry. That was fine by me. I just wanted to get on with this and get home. Everything seemed set, everything seemed to be in place, but you know what they say about the best laid plans…

ALL AROUND
THE HOUSES

No sooner had Olly come in to see me than she had to go
back to the hotel to send some emails to my insurance
company. Meanwhile I was laid up with Ragnar, who asked
me how I got into motorbikes. I told him about Jason and
that monkey bike, but the real introduction came from
my mate Tommy Rochford and his Maico 500. Back then
the only bikers I knew were the neighbours I grew up with.
One was Kaz who lived on a property across the river,
and the other was Tommy, whose dad looked after our
property and regularly sat down to lunch with our family. I
got into biking largely through Tommy and that Maico,
when he'd tear through the countryside as if the Garda
were after him.

I told Ragnar about my expeditions into the mountains
when I was a kid. I told him that though I'll always have
a problem with words, early on in my life my dad
recognised in me what he calls an 'innate visual intelligence'.
No matter how young I was, no matter where my wandering
took me, I always found my way home. I'd be gone long

enough for Mum and Dad to begin to worry, then I'd come walking across the lawn or up the drive, safely back from another adventure.

I wasn't always on my own on such adventures. One weekend the playwright Tom Stoppard was over with his son Oliver. There was plenty to do and explore as we had horses and the river, but there was also a quarry just beyond a field that marked the edge of the property. It had long since been dug out and nobody went there but us. It was a great place to doss about so I took Oliver. We did a bit of scrambling and some shallow climbs then I showed him how to get up one of the steeper walls. He followed me, moving where I did, but halfway up he froze. He just clung there, not moving up or down, so I climbed back down to where he was.

'Just take the next handhold,' I said.

He didn't move. He just looked at me with the kind of fear in his eyes that takes over when your muscles seize.

'Go on, Oliver,' I encouraged him. 'It's easy, just go for the next handhold.'

I showed him where it was but he didn't reach for it, so I told him to climb down again instead. But he couldn't do that either; he was rooted, frozen to that little ledge. I'd been up there more times than I could remember and I told him it wasn't steep enough to really fall; if he let go he could slide down (albeit quickly) on his bum. But he wasn't doing that either. In the end I told him to stay where he was and I'd go back to the house for help.

I did that, leaving the poor lad clinging to the rock wall, and set off to get my dad. Halfway home I saw Snowy, Telsche's horse, kicking her heels in a gallop and rolling over in the grass. I loved that horse; we all did. As I watched her all thought of Oliver went out of my head.

I wandered back to the house thinking I'd go to the kitchen and get something to eat. Dad was at the stables taking a brush to another horse and I told him I'd been watching Snowy.

'That horse,' he said, 'she won't take the bridle no matter what Telsche does.'

'You have to creep up on her,' I said. 'That's the only way to do it, creep up with a carrot or something.'

Dad went back to grooming and I set off towards the house.

'Charley?' Dad called after me. 'What did you do with Oliver?'

'Oh my God!' My hand was suddenly at my mouth.

Dad looked over, a little concerned. 'Where is he? What've you done?'

I was already running back the way I had come. 'He's in the quarry, Dad, he's stuck on a ledge!'

Dropping the brush, Dad ran after me. As we got to the quarry we spotted this disconsolate figure wandering towards us with tears in his eyes, covered in dust.

A little while later Olly came back to the ward and told me how she was getting on with the travel insurer. We required an air ambulance, which wasn't difficult to set up. We just had to confirm the date and the details of what would happen when we arrived back in London. In the meantime, Triumph told us they would pick up the tab for Olly's stay, which I was really grateful for. It was one less thing to worry about and really good of them, especially as they were hardly getting their money's worth from their bedridden ambassador.

I was in better spirits now things were starting to happen. I couldn't see the end of the road, but we were into the bends and there was a nice long straight ahead. The surgeon was pleased with the how the operations had gone given how complicated the break had been. He spoke to Olly and she made notes which would be useful when we got back to London:

Hand needs re-doing, needs a plate, head of metacarpal not back where it should be. As far as the ankle is concerned, keep elevated, get soft tissue to settle down.

This wasn't the first time she'd seen me injured. She'd been in Africa after I broke my hands and witnessed the lines of wounded riders laid out as if they'd been brought from a battlefield. The surgeon checked my blood again and the levels of haemoglobin had begun to rise, meaning I should be alright to fly by the following Tuesday lunchtime. In less than a week I'd be in King Edward VII Hospital under the care of the surgeon recommended by Katrine's friend, and then I could really begin my recovery. Or so I thought.

Late on Friday afternoon Olivia was contacted by my private healthcare company – and suddenly everything went to rat shit. They left it until almost 5pm, when their offices were about to close for the weekend, to tell us that I couldn't go to the King Edward VII after all. Because I was a victim of multiple trauma I had to be assessed by an NHS hospital and a treatment plan drawn up before I could be admitted to any private facility. The only other way I could go straight to King Edward VII was if my GP in London referred me. That wasn't going to happen; the surgery was about to close for the weekend and the GP couldn't refer me unless he'd physically examined me.

It was ridiculous. We had to confirm the air ambulance on Monday or we'd lose the slot and what they were asking was too much, given that it was the weekend. The plan we'd already made had been difficult enough for Olly to set up whilst liaising with Katrine in London. For some reason we'd assumed that a comprehensive private healthcare policy would provide a dedicated liaison in London. We thought someone would be contacting hospitals and doctors on our behalf, but apparently that's not the way it works. All the insurance company does is tick boxes. The patient has to provide the treatment plan, and the surgeons, consultants, anaesthetists and all have to be approved by the insurance company.

A bombshell had been dropped. Now we were fighting the clock from a foreign country, and over a weekend as well. If we didn't confirm the air ambulance in time it could be another week at least before we were allocated another slot. Olly got straight back on the phone and spoke to Katrine, then directly to her heart surgeon friend Jullien Gaer. He emailed the CEO of my insurer and the email was forwarded to their Clinical Operations Director. He was on holiday at the time with his children so I have no idea why it was sent to him. To his credit he emailed back immediately – but said he couldn't access the files remotely.

It seemed like a dead end. Olly was constantly calling and emailing, tearing her hair out, trying to deal with the fallout from what we'd been told. But in times like these, you never know what strange coincidence or lucky break will bring about your next step. In this case, it was cooking.

Right about now you're probably wondering what culinary expertise has got to do with an injured motorcycle adventurer, let alone finding them a way home. A couple of years back I was on *Celebrity MasterChef*. With Gregg Wallace assessing my skills in the kitchen I made it to the final and came a close runner-up. Because of this I had offered my culinary services at an auction raising money for Key4Life, the charity my wife volunteers for. The winning bidder had been someone called Stuart Fletcher, the CEO of another health insurance company entirely. I was due to cook for him and ten guests in a couple of days' time.

While my wife was chasing up options with hospitals, Billy was dealing with other issues caused by my accident. Since I wouldn't be able to make it to cook for Stuart, Billy was emailing to apologise, hopefully reschedule, and explain that I was laid up in hospital in Portugal. He took the opportunity to pick Stuart's brains on our dilemma with the insurance company.

Stuart wasted no time in calling his company's director of medical health benefits, Lorna Friedman. She's based in New York, but that didn't stop her pulling out all the stops for us that weekend. She put us in contact with a guy called Simon Ball who's the orthopaedic consultant surgeon at the Chelsea and Westminster hospital in London. After a multitude of emails and phone calls it was he who circumnavigated the politics.

It was a brilliant leap forward, and from a completely unexpected source. But there were still plenty of hurdles to jump before it could be confirmed that I'd be seen at the Chelsea and Westminster. It's one of five NHS trauma centres in London, and initially we were told that there weren't any available beds and also that a junior doctors' strike was planned for the day we got back. The situation looked pretty grim, but Simon said he would see what he could do. He was thinking that rather than just having me assessed there before transferring me to the King Edward VII, my treatment should all take place at the Chelsea and Westminster instead.

Meanwhile, Olly was trying to contact our local GP to see if there was any way we could email him the details from Portugal and get a phone referral rather than a physical examination, meaning I could go straight to the King Edward VII. I have to say that was my preferred option, but it was the weekend and the GP wouldn't be in until Monday. If there was any chance he could be persuaded to make that kind of referral, the call would have to happen first thing – otherwise we'd lose the slot with the air ambulance.

There was yet another complication for good measure. When it came to the NHS, Olly was told that I had to be admitted to the hospital closest to where we live. That was Charing Cross, but they weren't able to deal with the seriousness of my injuries. They did offer me a bed until one became available at the Chelsea and Westminster, but both my ankle and wrist seriously needed treatment. I didn't want to have to lie in one hospital just waiting to go elsewhere, nothing being done surgically to help my recovery.

So we were fighting on a whole stack of fronts; the hospitals, the GP, various emails flying back and forth in order to secure a bed and get the treatment plan the insurance company insisted upon. We sent over the notes so that Simon at the Chelsea and Westminster could formulate the plan, and he reiterated the idea that the treatment should take place there. That way he could oversee the situation with input from foot, ankle and hand specialists. He told us he could cut through the red tape that was threatening the booking we'd made with the air ambulance and, given there was a private wing, I could go straight there with no need to take a bed from an NHS patient.

It had been a fraught weekend. At times Olly was literally tearing her hair out, and it all kicked off because we weren't given the full information in the first place. When I look at the number of emails going back and forth I can barely believe it — but thankfully, finally, we knew I was going home. Also I already had experience with one of the surgeons from the Chelsea and Westminster: hand specialist Rupert Eckersley, the same guy who'd worked on me after the injuries I sustained at the Dakar.

It was settled. After a manic 48 hours, we were able to confirm the air ambulance with a flight to Biggin Hill followed by ground transportation to the Chelsea and Westminster. Here and now I want to say a massive thank you to Jullien Gaer and Simon Ball, Stuart Fletcher and Lorna Friedman for all their efforts in ensuring I received the best treatment. Without their help and advice I'd probably still be languishing in that room with poor old Ragnar.

We weren't back in London yet though; there was still so much that could go wrong. After the insurance company's shock announcement we were on edge in case of any more complications. My poor wife had so much to deal with in difficult circumstances in a foreign country — and her only respite came in the form of Ana. Ana, the wonderful woman who had stopped to help me by the side of the road. It turned out she worked in the same hotel I'd been staying in with the boys from Triumph.

It felt like we had unfinished business. We had been thrown into such an intense moment together, a kind of intimacy and emotional intensity that most people never share. She'd helped me, comforted me and sat for ages supporting my injured leg – but then the ambulance arrived and she wasn't needed anymore, and I was whisked away. I found out later that she had been quite upset about the whole thing, and when she and her husband came to visit me I was delighted.

Ana sat with me for some time. She told me all about her family; how her daughter was going to university but it was hard to get work in that part of Portugal right now. She was coping with the fact her daughter might be some distance away, and it bothered her but there didn't seem to be any choice. She told me she'd been thinking about what happened ever since she saw me carried off in the ambulance. She wanted to make sure I was alright – and I told her I got that, I knew why she needed to see me. I understood totally because many years ago I experienced a similar thing.

It happened not long after I started dating Olly. She had a world trip planned with six months in Australia. I wasn't working on any films at the time, so we ended up making the trip together.

We were in Sydney for a while, then travelled up the coast to Queensland where we stayed at Jason's mother's place near Port Douglas. Though now sadly passed away, Diane Cilento was a wonderful woman and actress, and she made us really welcome. I'd been there once before with Jason and Hopie Davis, who went to school with my sister Daisy. (She's married to my dad now, which is a bit bizarre, but that's another story.) We made sure we covered the cost of our stay by doing odd jobs around the place. One day we'd been up to Mossman to shop for food and were on our way back in the car. It's a beautiful part of the world where the road hugs the coast.

As we made our way back to Diane's place I saw this guy running up the road waving his arms. We stopped, of course, and he told me a car had run off the road a little further south and was in the creek under a bridge. He took off to find a phone and we drove down to the bridge where we could see the car upended underneath. I jumped out and rushed down to find that the creek was more of a wash than a full-blown river. But that didn't change the fact that the car was upside down with the engine still running, and there was smoke coming off the bonnet.

I found a woman trapped by her seatbelt in the driver's seat, in great distress. There was no sign of anyone else. As calmly as I could, I asked if she was alright. She was incoherent, really confused. She kept going on about her kids, asking me where they were, saying they had been in the car.

I couldn't see anyone except her, and the car was a wreck – the windows were smashed and the roof partially caved in. The whole back half was soaked in reeds and vegetation and there was no sign of any children. Not only that, it was Australia: there could easily be spiders, snakes, crocodiles – all manner of deadly things lurking close by. I have to say, knee-deep in water, I was as conscious of that as I was the woman trapped at the steering wheel.

She was still asking about her kids and I thought that maybe she'd taken a bang on the head and that must've confused her. I decided she'd probably dropped her children off somewhere before the car ran off the road, but now could not remember. I did my best to keep her calm but she was getting more and more panicked, trying to look behind to see if her children were in the back, while all the time the seatbelt was so tight against her neck that her face was an intense puce colour.

I knew I couldn't let the situation get out of hand. If she carried on like that she was likely to slip into a complete panic; so I told her the kids were fine, they were safe and well and we had to concentrate on what had happened to her. I wanted to get that seatbelt off her but I didn't know whether she had any internal injuries and I didn't want to make matters worse. I hesitated, torn.

But the belt was strangling her and the car was smoking, and I was starting to worry about fire and leaking petrol. I asked her if she could move her hands and feet, and she could. I asked her to move her head from side to side, and she could do that alright. By now she was begging me to get her out, and I had a Leatherman multi-tool on my belt so I used it to cut the seatbelt. Then, very carefully, I managed to get her out of the car, and helped her up to the side of the road where Olivia was waiting.

The woman was grazed all over her arms and face from the broken glass but she was moving alright – I knew then that cutting her out had been the right thing. By this time the young guy we had seen arrived to tell us an ambulance was on its way. There was still no sign of any children though, so I spoke to Olly and she went off to talk to some people from another car. The ambulance turned up, and as the paramedics took over I explained what I'd done. They told me that my decision was fine; in cases like this it was always 50–50 and even they usually went by gut feeling.

That's when I found out there had been kids in the car when it crashed; two of them. Thankfully they'd managed to get out as soon as the car hit the water, and had hooked up with the young guy we'd seen running up the road. They were waiting further down the hill which is why we hadn't seen them. Their mother had been too confused to remember that they'd told her they were going for help. I watched as the paramedics loaded her into the ambulance and suddenly I was left to come down from the rush of adrenalin, my part in her rescue over.

But, just like Ana, I couldn't get the moment out of my head. I knew she'd been pretty banged up. I knew she'd been taken to hospital so a couple days later I went to visit her.

After they'd visited me Ana and her husband met up with Olly, taking her into town to show her around. I tried to get a little sleep. That wasn't easy. It was almost a week since I'd come off the bike. I was itchy, restless and desperate to get back to London. Though if I'd known what awaited me, I wouldn't have been in such a hurry.

PART TWO

24 February – 11 March 2016:
Chelsea and Westminster Hospital,

London, England

LONDON

The doctors came by on Monday morning to make one last assessment. They assured me all was well and I was good to go, save the requirement for a thrombotic injection. This was protein and iron to keep my blood thin because the last thing I needed on the flight home was to develop deep vein thrombosis. Everything had been confirmed, the paperwork was ready for the crew of the air ambulance, and I was relieved that my week in this hospital at least was almost over and we'd soon be back in London. I said my goodbyes to Ragnar. Confirmation of the timings came through to Olly via email, so there it was reassuringly spelled out in black and white. The plane would arrive in Faro on 23 February at 12.10pm. A Portuguese ground ambulance would bring two doctors to the hospital and they would transport us back to the airport for a scheduled take-off at 3pm.

So on Tuesday morning, exactly a week after the crash, I was back on another gurney – though not in so much pain as I had been the last time. I was grateful for that; and in as good a mood as I could be given the circumstances, I was wheeled out to the ambulance and transferred to their gurney.

Forty minutes later we were at Faro airport heading through the customs checkpoint, which was well away from the terminal. It was little more than a barrier where our passports were checked, and all was very quick and easy. We got to the plane, a small machine which the crew wasn't sure could accommodate Olly and all our luggage, but thankfully we got everything and everyone in.

The doctors asked if I wanted to take some oral morphine before we took off, but I told them I'd be alright. We were about to enter a pressurised cabin and I had no idea if that would affect the amount of pain I was in or not. They told me not to be a martyr, so I relented, took some and settled down. With the pilots in charge up ahead, Olly was finally able to get a little downtime. It was quite the trip for my mind on morphine, all colours and lights, a little bit of psychedelia on the way back to British winter. I recall one delicious moment; the lights were low and Olivia was in silhouette against a perfect moon. The image brought a sense of calm to the whole situation. I did wonder about her, though. I was taking up most of the room, then there were the doctors, the luggage…it made the cabin pretty cramped. Olly doesn't do well in confined spaces so I asked if she was alright. She told me she was fine as long as she knew where the door was. Her calm, like my silence, comes through telling herself that a door can be opened and she can get out at any time. Though I'm not sure that would be such a good idea at 30,000 feet.

We landed briefly in Jersey to refuel, and I'm sure that's because aviation fuel is cheaper in the Channel Islands than it is at home. Pretty soon we were on our way again and a little while later we made our approach to Biggin Hill Airport, just south of London.

It was early evening when we arrived and made the relatively short transfer to Chelsea and Westminster Hospital. It was great to be back in Britain; I didn't even mind the fact that it was February and there was no heating whatsoever in the ambulance. I was feeling good about where I was, about where we were headed. After the unrelenting hassle Olivia had been through at the weekend, all the discussions with so many different consultants and doctors, I felt that the familiarity of this hospital would be a good thing. That might sound odd, but I knew the place well. We all did. Both our daughters had been born there, my mother (who was ill for many years) was in and out of the place all the time, and Katrine and Daisy were just around the corner.

The first person I saw was Simon Ball, the consultant orthopaedic surgeon who had helped us so much from afar over the weekend. He came into my room that evening to introduce himself and look at the X-rays Olly had brought from Portugal. They showed a pair of screws just below my left knee, and a plate running the length of what remained of the tibia that was held in place by four additional screws. He said we would talk more in the morning and went away to make notes that he would pass to the specialists he planned to bring in. I got the notes later – apparently he found me alert and orientated (well, that's a first). I seemed to be comfortable and all my observations were stable. My

Glasgow Coma Scale score was 15/15 – that meant all my faculties were functioning (another first). There was no sign of any neurological problems with either my upper or lower limbs, nothing wrong with my vision; and my spine was normal, as was my face. (I know what you're thinking. Don't even go there).

The consultant noted that I had no drug allergies and was a social smoker. I'm not anymore. One of the first things they told me was that to regrow bone you needed to avoid carbon monoxide. Every drag I took on a cigarette whilst in recovery would inhibit that bone growth because the absorption of carbon monoxide was instant. Needless to say, I haven't had a cigarette since.

What I wasn't aware of then, however, were the problems the consultant could see with my left leg. I got the notes later and the literal diagnosis was:

> *Complex open left tibial fracture*
> *Right closed fracture dislocation ankle*
> *Fracture right index metacarpal*
> *Raise creatine kinase.*

That was followed with an abbreviation of the procedures undertaken by the surgeon in Portugal:

> *Left tibia ORIF and washout and closure of wound*
> *Right ankle ORIF*
> *K-wire fixation right index metacarpal*

That had all taken place the day of the accident, and now Simon needed to formulate a treatment plan. A surgeon called Andy Roche was to review my ankle and Rupert Eckersley my right hand. As I mentioned before, I already knew Eckersley because it was he who operated on my other hand after the crash that ended my race to Dakar (we'll talk more about that later). Other than the surgery I was to have a series of X-rays as well as a CT scan on the ankle. They would also keep a close eye on the wound to my left leg in terms of the skin cell condition and refer me to a plastic surgeon.

It all sounded a little daunting and I was beginning to feel a bit nervous. Somehow I'd convinced myself that what they'd done in Portugal was enough and it was just a case of recuperation. The reality was that the worst was still to come, though I wasn't aware of it then.

By now most of our friends knew what had happened, and many of them were already planning to visit. Ewan was in LA but he'd been on the phone and was very concerned. Jason called with news that he'd be in the country as his new movie was opening the Edinburgh Festival, and he'd come and see me as soon as he could.

If it hadn't been for the consultant's solemn demeanour there would have been relief all round. We were back in London. I was in familiar and comfortable surroundings and Olly could go home to her own bed every night instead of a hotel. Future projects were on my mind again, and I was talking and thinking about nothing but a full recovery. Before I took on the Darien Gap there was the bike tour from Melbourne to Sydney, and there was no way I'd make that now. I'd already spoken to Billy about what we might do and there was a possibility a couple of friends could help out. Ross Noble, a mate and mad-keen biker, was on a stand-up comedy tour in Oz so he might be able to do something. Then there were the natives, actor Eric Bana and also motorcycle racer Mick Doohan, five-time 500cc World Championship winner, who we could possibly call on as well. I was hoping to be able to make it to South America for the inaugural expedition in September, but we'd have to wait and see. I still wasn't totally sure how the recovery would go; it all depended on how the surgeons assessed what the Portuguese had done with my leg.

Despite those sojourns I took as a kid, I'm not a quiet person by nature. I love company and being surrounded by people. My wife always jokes that when I was on film sets, rather than retreat to my trailer between takes I'd remain on the set helping one of the hands with one thing or another. Still, when the shit really does hit the fan I always seek solace in silence.

Lying there in my room after everyone had gone, the lights very low, my mind started to wander. I was thinking about hospitals and how whenever I'm anywhere near one I can't help but think about my sister Telsche. Writer, actress, wonderful mother to my niece Daphne; she was seven years older than me and though we lost her 20 years ago, she nearly didn't make it to school age.

Before I was born Dad and Mum lived in the New Forest where Dad was making documentaries for the BBC. There was a small pond in the garden; one day when Telsche was a toddler she tripped over and fell in. She hit her head and lay with her face in the water, and that's where my mother found her.

Dad was in the house at the time and he describes hearing this horrific primordial wail. He rushed outside where my mother was on her knees holding Telsche. Mum was broken, sobbing. Telsche had no pulse, her face was the colour of chalk and she wasn't breathing. In those days the method of resuscitating drowning victims wasn't widely known, but there had been a piece about it in the newspaper just a couple of days before – a small diagram that miraculously Dad had seen and thought he could remember. Easing back Telsche's head he opened her mouth and breathed into her lungs. Nothing happened. He did it again and again, trying to keep calm, but still nothing happened. He repeated the process yet again, though all seemed lost – and suddenly she spluttered. She was coughing hard and Dad tipped her over so she could bring up the water in her lungs. She had come back to life, and from that day on she told everyone that she'd been born twice: the first time by her mother, and the second time by her dad.

Dad saved Telsche's life and I was beginning to think I might need someone to save mine. My entire existence revolved around being on a motorbike and though I was being my usual confident, positive self, right now my future was impossible to predict.

The consultant was back in my room with the treatment plan at 7.10 the following morning. A youngish guy from Ireland, Simon was easy to talk to and I immediately took a liking to him. He's a knee man mostly, specialising in sports-related injuries, and he'd captained the University Football Club at Cambridge. While we chatted he told me he'd actually played semi-professionally, but his studies took over and he concentrated on medicine. As far as I was concerned, after all the rigmarole and uncertainty in trying to get the right hospital and care he was a perfect fit, and I think he was looking forward to the challenge. He was already considering what had been done in Portugal and was pretty frank when he told me he wasn't sure it was the best thing.

I felt sucker-punched. That was the last thing I wanted to hear. Simon was concerned about the plate they'd inserted because when he massaged the leg it didn't feel very secure. It moved around as if it was held in place by nothing but soft tissue. He was also concerned about infection and made a point of telling me it was something that would haunt the recovery process until the bone had fully regrown. Though they'd been scrupulous in Portugal, the plate itself might be a problem. Apparently the downside of fitting metal inside the leg is that infection has the propensity to travel. If a bug found its way to the top of the wound it would make its way down the length of the plate and infect the bottom of the leg, where the flow of blood is at its weakest.

The consultant told me we'd know more when I'd been examined by the leg man he was going to refer me to. While I tried to take in the implications of what he'd said, he arranged for Andy Roche (the ankle specialist) to take a look at what they'd done with the pin. He also contacted Rupert Eckersley about my hand. As I mentioned, Rupert had worked on me after the Dakar but he'd also treated my dad. A few years ago, Dad fell over and broke his wrist and it was Rupert who attended him. Pure chance, but he recognised the Boorman name and asked if we were related.

Rupert saw me later that morning – the door flew open and he came steaming in. 'Charley,' he said, peering at the pins sticking out of my right hand, 'I hope you haven't ruined all my good work.'

'No,' I replied, holding up my left. 'This is the hand you operated on.'

He looked more closely and could see that the pins had forced my index finger off at an angle so it was lying crosswise under the middle one. He wasn't happy. The pins had only been designed to keep the metacarpal in place until it could be operated on in London. He told me they needed to come out right now otherwise the bone was going to set in an unnatural position. I wasn't delighted to hear that; far from it. I'd already had three operations in the last week and was feeling pretty beaten up. I told him I didn't want another anaesthetic today – could it wait till tomorrow?

'Anaesthetic,' he said, 'what anaesthetic? You don't need an anaesthetic. We'll do it here and now.'

I looked up at him in horror. 'What do you mean?'

'Charley,' he said. 'I've got a nurse coming in to cast a splint for your hand. We can't get that cast in place with pins in the bone so best we whip them out.'

He explained that the nurse would heat a sheet of plastic so it was malleable and could be shaped into a right-angled splint to fit the underside of my fingers. The nurse arrived promptly a few minutes later with the materials, a water bath and what looked like an industrial hairdryer. She started setting up, and Rupert reached for my hand with the kind of smile only a surgeon can muster. It was like someone asking a reluctant dog for its paw. Before I knew what was going on I had the nurse on one side and the surgeon on the other, then another nurse came in with what appeared to be massive pair of pliers. The whole room seemed to reverberate as she laid them down with a cold metal clang.

From the tranquillity of being in a private room I suddenly was in some crazy scene from the *Little Shop of Horrors*. Gurgling water and hot air, a mad scientist looming over my bed with a pair of stainless steel pliers – I started to shrink back against the bedhead, red-faced and sweating. Panic rose; a hint of vomit in my throat, tears in my eyes...

Rupert looked at me as if I was a blubbering baby.

'Oh, for God's sake, Charley,' he said. 'I have patients as young as six coming in and I just pull out the pins. Man up will you, for God's sake.' He grabbed the pliers and started hauling on the pins, while I tried to hold still if not pull back with my hand. Finally, after a little bit of to-ing and fro-ing, and the odd whimper escaping my lips, the pins were out.

I was left with a brand new splint and my hand bent forward at the wrist to spread the fingers. My hand looked a bit bizarre at that angle but there was no real pain post pin-pulling, so all I could do was lick my wounded pride as I tried to deal with the humiliation of being compared with a six-year-old. At that moment my friend Russ Malkin turned up complete with a stack of six-year-old magazines. He took one look at my hand – then bent one of his own into the same posture and fisted his other on his hip.

'I'm a little teapot, short and stout…'

'Shut up, Russ,' I said.

When I say the magazines were six years old, I mean they were the sort aimed at people aged six and upwards: *The Beano*, *The Dandy*, that kind of thing. Clearly, after knowing me as long as he has, Russ is only too aware of my reading skills. He was there to see how I was, but also to talk about the fact that our attempt at crossing the Darien Gap had had to be shelved for the time being. He'd spoken to Channel 5 and was hopeful that the show would still go ahead, just not until the spring of 2017. That was a year from now and I was convinced I'd be fit enough.

Russ left me with the comics and they seemed a little banal, even for me – but as I leafed through them I realised they were just a front for one of his jokes. Hidden between the *Beano* and *Dandy* were a couple of other magazines that were far from suitable for kids.

When Olly came in a little later she saw them lying in the pile with the comics and mentioned tactfully that we might want to get rid of them. I told her I'd have already chucked them in the bin if I could have reached but it was too far from the bed. Olly stuffed them in for me, one of those flip up affairs with a disposable liner, and that's the last I thought of them.

I did, however, see them again. The next morning, one of the orderlies came in, a fellow named Mohammad who would be there every day. He swept the floor and we chatted, then he unhooked the bin liner to take the rubbish away. To my horror I discovered that, far from being thick black plastic, the bin liner was transparent. The magazines were lying in such a way that two pairs of naked breasts were abundantly visible. Mohammad hadn't noticed; he carried the bag swinging at his side with the mags facing out, completely oblivious to the odd looks he was getting as he exited my room and headed for the lift.

We all had a titter about it, a couple of light-hearted moments that I desperately needed while I tried to dissect all that the consultant had said about my leg. But the respite didn't last long. His fears were echoed and then exacerbated when I met the surgeon he recommended. Grey-haired and no-nonsense, Dinesh Nathwani arrived, and what he said chilled me to my shattered tibia.

Before I spoke to him though, I talked to Billy.

So, what does Billy do? Well, he works with me in various capacities; we do theatre tours together and he's a big part of my 'Ride with Charley Boorman' tours. I've called him a sort of manager, but it's hard to put any kind of indicative title on him – he's just Billy Ward, another mad-keen biker, and a funnier, more off-the-wall guy you couldn't meet. I ran into him a few years back when he worked in the IT industry and I was doing some speaking engagements with a portable amp and a mic in the wake of *Long Way Round*. He came forward, introduced himself, and promptly told me it was crap. He said the people at the back couldn't hear, and if I gave him the opportunity he'd show me a much better way of presenting. For weeks afterwards he kept badgering me on the phone, telling me that if I let him put together a video package we could fill theatres. In the end I said he should come and talk to me, then I called Russ. I wanted him along for another opinion in case this Scouser was full of shit.

It turned out that he was, and yet he wasn't. I know that doesn't seem to make any sense – but then most of the time, neither does Billy. We had a meeting and he turned up with a 'Theatre Producer' business card he'd only just had made. Russ wanted to know about return on investment percentages and timescales of that return. Looking a little blank, Billy talked about cost per head and as many people as we could cram into the theatre, when the truth was he'd never actually been in a theatre, never mind produced a show. There was something about him I liked though – probably the way he was clearly winging it, and in the end we gave it a shot. He was as good as his word and put together the kind of theatre tour he'd been talking about and later we set up the 'Ride with Charley Boorman' expeditions.

I called him as I lay in my room at the Chelsea and Westminster. We had to figure out a way we could keep our clients happy, given that they'd paid to ride with me and I wasn't going to be anywhere near Australia. It was the first trip where Billy and I would've been on Triumphs, a two-week expedition with 30 guests, and we had to come up with some compensation. It had been on Billy's mind ever since he learned how serious my injury was. Initially he thought I'd be able to fly over with a pair of crutches and accompany the tour in the support vehicle. That way I'd be there for the craic in the hotels every night, where I like to regale our guests with tales of terror from the Dakar and the expeditions with Ewan.

As time went on, however, it became clear that I wouldn't be there in any capacity. Billy commented that the real difficulty of repatriating someone after a bike accident had come home to him in a way he had never been aware of before. We'd done it on a couple of occasions during the trips in Africa, but that had been from the perspective of the tour guide, not the victim. As far as we were concerned it had just been a case of getting the injured party on a plane. But when you're the person who's come off the bike, it's much more complicated than any of us had realised.

Given my condition, I had no choice but to leave the mess of dealing with the Australian trip to Billy, and he started to think about the contacts we had out there. He'd already Tweeted some stuff about the accident so the clients were aware it had happened, and made sure they were kept up-to-date with the situation and how it would affect the tour – and especially that we were going to make sure their experience wasn't diminished. Obviously the last thing we wanted was any of them bailing on us (and I want to say a massive thanks to all of them for their support).

The most important thing was to offer them something or someone who could suitably take my place. It's true that when you work in the kind of world I do you meet a fair few celebs, and we were already thinking about Eric Bana and Mick Doohan. Eric's been a mate since I received an email from him a few years ago. He had seen the *Long Way* stuff on TV and likes to ride bikes. He knew I was going to be in Oz so he invited me for dinner one night, and that's how we became friends. When Billy got in touch with him about our Australian tour concerns, Eric agreed to have dinner with the guests in Melbourne. He couldn't commit to riding with them because he was due on a movie set and was waiting to find out the dates, but was more than happy to meet the group, have a team photo and that kind of thing.

As it turned out, however, he had to be on set earlier than he'd envisioned and wasn't able to be there after all. With that plan shelved Billy got in touch with Mick Doohan, a biking icon not just in Australia but around the world. Mick had been the up-and-coming racer during one of the most competitive 500cc eras of all time. It was the two-stroke days of the early 1990s when he pitted his wits against the likes of Wayne Rainey and Eddie Lawson, before winning five world titles in a row. Even more impressively, all those titles were achieved after he'd suffered massive leg injuries in a crash at Assen. The loss of blood to one leg was so bad he had to have both sewn together in order to stop the doctors having to amputate. Once the blood supply had been fully re-established they separated the legs again and he eventually returned to the track, and then the podium.

Mick said he'd be happy to fly down to Sydney and meet the party for dinner at the end of the tour, which would be a real bonus for the guests. I was heartened to have that in the locker while Billy was doing his best to get someone else to take my place on the ride. I mentioned Ross Noble before, and the fact he just happened to be on tour down under. Billy is Ross's tour manager and likes to tell me that he should've been along with him taking advantage of all the hotel perks rather than picking up the pieces after me. He knew Ross's schedule and that Ross is always gagging to ride motorbikes. Billy phoned him up; Ross agreed to ride in my place for a couple of days.

But we weren't going to stop there. We still had a joker up our sleeve: it was just a question of getting him to agree to fly out, and make sure there were no hitches along the way. I remember when we started the second *By Any Means* expedition from Sydney to Tokyo, and a certain globe-trotting cameraman had gone down a storm with the crowd that had gathered to see us off. Actually I'm pretty sure he got a bigger cheer than I did. I'm talking about Claudio von Planta, the cameraman who filmed Ewan and me during *Long Way Round* and *Long Way Down*. Billy gave him a call and tentatively asked him if there was any chance he could take my place. Initially, Claudio's response was 'possibly'. With the next call, it was 'maybe'. Finally, we heard that one magic word we'd been waiting for.

Fantastic. Lying in hospital and hearing that news come through, I began to think we might actually get away with it. But then we're talking about Claudio von Planta, and those of you who know our history will be aware that he doesn't come without complications. Don't get me wrong, there's no ego with Claudio; nothing untoward in his manner or in his dealings with us at all. He's a good friend. What I mean is there's always something that seems to get in the way, some detail nobody thought about, that stops him actually being ready at the beginning of an expedition. The lack of a bike licence for *Long Way Round* for instance, or the fact that the licence had expired when we set out from John O'Groats to Cape Town on *Long Way Down*.

As it turned out, this was to be no different. Claudio gets about quite a bit in his role as cameraman and photojournalist. Historically he's ruffled a few political feathers and was one of the first people ever to interview Osama Bin Laden. As I mentioned, he'd been with us in Australia for the second *By Any Means* tour and that was the crux of the problem. When he left the country he'd not had his passport stamped. How that happened I don't know, but when he applied for a visa for this trip he received a letter telling him his application had been accepted. He took that to mean the visa would be granted, and thought no more of it – but it just meant the application had been received.

It all went tits-up when he got to the airport and tried to board the plane. Bear in mind Billy was in Melbourne by that point; the tour was about to begin, and he was waiting on a phone call from Claudio.

'Hi, Billy, it's Claudio. I'm at the airport.'

'Great, great,' Billy said. 'I'll come down and pick you up.'

'No, not that airport, I'm still at Heathrow. They won't let me on the plane.'

I knew it had been too good to be true and perhaps Billy did too, because we hadn't actually told the clients. We'd kept Claudio's attendance as a surprise we'd reveal just as we were about to get going. Billy's newsletter had gone out with the Mick Doohan and Ross Noble attendance, but we'd said nothing about our other star man. That was probably just as well because there he was, stuck at the desk in London, the authorities telling him he couldn't get on the plane as his passport and visa were not in order. Over the next couple of days we tried everything to sort it out, but to no avail. The clock was ticking, firm plans had to be made, and in the end, they could not include Claudio.

LIMB SALVATION

While all this was going on I was only a day into my UK repatriation with at least two operations imminent. The consultant came by to tell me he'd arranged for some specialists who work hand-in-glove to assess my left leg, but it would mean a move to the Charing Cross Hospital after my initial operations. One I've already mentioned – Dinesh Nathwani, the consultant orthopaedic surgeon – and the other guy was Jon Simmons, a consultant plastic surgeon. I met Dinesh first, and while I'm sure he didn't mean to alarm me, by the time he'd imparted the details after his assessment of my injury I was a quivering wreck.

He gave me a bit of background on who he was, how he'd worked in the orthoplastic reconstruction service since he was first appointed consultant in 2004. He told me that he performs the surgery in tandem with Jon Simmons, as well as four other orthopaedic specialists and four more plastic surgeons. Dinesh and Jon are in theatre at the same time whereas most such surgeons are in different wings or even different hospitals. Some time ago they decided that, since one aspect of the reconstruction process directly affects the other, the best result for the patient would be achieved if they were in theatre together. Much of what they do is to try and reconstruct shattered limbs – usually from bike accidents like mine. Dinesh told me that the treatments they've developed over the last five years have greatly enhanced their rate of what he referred to as 'limb salvation'.

Jesus, just the term alone was enough to strip the blood from my cheeks. I lay there looking up at this guy as he pointed out what had been done in Portugal, how he wasn't happy with it, and what complications could occur.

'That's the worst that can happen,' he said. 'Losing the limb. But with what we propose hopefully it should be avoided. There is no guarantee though; it's a long process and the key is bone growth and a blood supply to the bone. The bone growth will be checked at 12 weeks to see if the tibia is fusing in the way we want it to, and that's the critical moment. You can call that D-Day if you want, because if the bone is still alive and fusing correctly then everything should be alright.' The expression in his eyes seemed to dull a little. 'If it hasn't, we might need a bone graft. That would be from the base of your leg, or maybe we could take it from your hip. Either way it would entail soft tissue and muscle graft, though my colleague will tell you more about that. Of course, we have to be mindful of infection because that brings the threat of amputation every step of the way.'

I was stunned, gobsmacked; this was the last thing I'd expected. Bone from my hip or even the base of my shin, muscle graft, blood vessels…amputation…I could hardly take it in. It was all delivered to me in a deadpan, no-

nonsense fashion, each word hitting me blow by bitter blow. As I lay there reeling my mind skipped out; I remembered talking to Ian Hutchinson about his crash at Silverstone a few years ago when they were contemplating taking his leg off.

'It's a bad break.' Dinesh's voice penetrated the fog that surrounded my thoughts. 'The one good thing is that's it's relatively close to the knee, which is better than lower down. The closer to the ankle, the harder it is to deal with, because the blood has further to travel. We stand a better chance of saving the leg when the break is higher up.' He moved around the bed and began to massage my shin. 'The plate they inserted in Portugal isn't stable. I think my colleague already pointed that out?'

He had. And now I could actually see the metal plate moving under the heavily stitched skin.

'The leg isn't aligned properly,' Dinesh went on. 'I think we might need to remove the plate and start again. Right now, there's a higher chance of infection and you're probably aware that bugs use metal to travel.' He paused for a moment. 'Whatever happens, you've lost substantial amounts of bone…and if we're going to save this leg, you're going to need major reconstructive surgery.'

With that he left. I sat there staring at Olly, absolutely no colour in my face. To be perfectly honest the shock was so great that as I write this I cannot remember the exact sequence of events. It might be that conversation took place a couple of days before the operation, but it might have been the same day. My wife thinks the latter, but my recollection is so hazy, I'm not sure. It doesn't really matter. The bottom line was, having flown home thinking my leg was pinned and healing nicely, I'd been hit with this.

I was in a cold sweat, facing at least one more operation then months of rehab before I even knew if what they were proposing had worked or not. On top of that I wasn't totally sure what exactly they were proposing and, until they opened me up, neither were they. The prospect of walking again seemed so remote that I had to choke back tears.

I tried to be positive. I told myself to deal with this. I focused on the practicalities and the fact that Dinesh had talked about a Taylor Spatial Frame. It's an external cage that fits around your leg where the good bone above and below the wound is secured with pins. I knew that's what Ian Hutchinson had been fitted with, and he'd come through a whole stack of operations and wasn't just walking; he was riding a motorbike and winning races on the Isle of Man.

The pins work from the outside in, allowing the fragments of bone that remained set in soft tissue to knit with wires so they could begin to reattach. The bone will remember where it was supposed to be, then hopefully fuse and begin to regrow. But it was all a little too much, a little too scientific to absorb right then and I lay back trying not to allow panic to set in. There's no feeling quite like being out of control. I was helpless – and it was not going to be over any time soon.

The notes were written up, including everything Dinesh had said. I was given a copy and I sat propped up against the pillows looking through the pages, the words swimming around then popping up in places where they shouldn't have been. I think that was maybe more the shock and painkillers I was on rather than anything to do with dyslexia though, because I can read just fine these days thanks to all the assistance I had as a kid.

Dyslexia is not all about reading: it's actually about how your brain works. Even now I find it hard to think chronologically. I know I need to do something and plan it, but literally minutes later I've forgotten all about it and moved onto something else. It wasn't helped by the fact that school wasn't a fixed entity in my life. Part of the reason I spend so much time on the road now is because that's how it's always been. Whenever Dad was on location he would take us with him, and in those early days the only time we weren't all together is when he made *Hell in the Pacific* when I was a toddler. Our family was based in LA back then, but filming would be from an island called Palau in the South Pacific. Dad was directing, and my mum Christel was designing costumes. Dad never made a movie without us all being around but this was a little different – most of the time the crew would be based on the island, where there were no emergency facilities, but plenty of bugs, mosquitos and general threat of disease. Dad and Mum decided that Daisy and I were just too young to be subjected to that, and the decision was made to leave us with some people Dad refers to as 'a wonderfully gothic

American couple', Mr and Mrs Miller, good friends they had known ever since Dad started working in LA. I didn't understand what was going on or why, only that my Mum wasn't there and neither was my Dad. My older sisters weren't there; it was just Daisy and me. That was traumatic at first but we soon adapted. Something about that experience must have dug deep into my psyche, regardless – it's my earliest memory.

Apart from that, though, we were always together, often on one movie set or another. As a child I was in and out of different schools all the time, both in Ireland and the UK. One of those schools was St Gerard's in Bray, County Wicklow, where I remember having to recite my times tables with my palm out so the teacher could slap me with a ruler if I made a mistake. It wasn't just me, it was all the children, and it's the most ridiculous approach to teaching I can think of. Make a mistake and you're slapped – it's hardly confidence-inspiring, and it would be unheard of today.

Back then I'd be in school for a while, then away on a film set somewhere with tutors teaching me and my sisters while we appeared as extras. I think Dad already knew that any form of academic qualifications would be beyond me so he made sure I was exposed to the world he worked in as much as he could. That said, when he made *Deliverance* in 1971 most of my time was spent with his driver racing around in a jeep where he taught me to shoot a gun. (I don't mean a rifle – I was only five – I mean that favoured American pastime of shooting road signs with the pistol he carried under the seat.)

Whenever I was home I'd be riding the DT100 Yamaha I'd finally acquired after waiting so long for it to come. I was about 11 or 12, it was the first proper motorbike I owned, and marked a new step in my adventures; whereas before I'd crossed the river to explore the world on foot, I was now doing it on a motorbike. I got used to off-road riding long before I was anywhere near tarmac, blatting through the green lanes with Tommy Rochford or Kaz Balinski. I mentioned them earlier; Kaz was the guy who lived just across the river. His parents were seriously rich and he always had a better bike than I did. He even had his own motocross track. I'm serious; a decent-sized circuit in a field his parents owned that abutted the shallowest part of the river, where we could walk across or ride our bikes. I did that all the time and Kaz and I would spend hours, days even, perfecting slides and jumps, pulling wheelies and cultivating skills that I would eventually use to an extent I could only have dreamed about back then.

It wasn't a full-blown motocross bike, but that DT did everything I asked of it and it's still in production today, albeit in a different form. First brought out as a 250 in 1968, it was a road bike you could ride on the dirt. It had high lift mudguards front and back so it looked like a motocrosser. A two-stroke of course, so there's no engine braking, it had a top speed of about 90mph.

I bought it with the money I'd earned as an extra in *The First Great Train Robbery*. (That's the film made in 1979 – nothing to do with Ronnie Biggs.) Sean Connery played Edward Pierce, a master thief who robs the gold train as it runs from London to Folkestone. The cargo was meant to be payment for British troops fighting in the Crimean War, and the movie is based on a true story. My first paying role; all I had to do was shin up a lamp post and hang there for a minute or two. Nobody else wanted to do it and there'd been talk of bringing in a stuntman. I was scared of words on a page but not much else, so I volunteered.

I didn't get paid very much but I was only about 11 so it didn't matter. What mattered was my first bike – so I gave all the money to Dad and he added the rest that was needed to buy the Yamaha. The day it was delivered to the house I remember getting up at the crack of dawn and waiting at the end of the drive all day.

I've still got it in a barn at my dad's house. A few years ago I got it going and taught my daughters to ride in the very place where I had first ridden. Doone and Kinvara weren't very old back then, and it was a real moment of serendipity. I throw a leg over that saddle whenever I visit my dad's house. Or at least…I did. Back in the hospital bed, drowning in the news they'd shaken me with, I knew that throwing a leg over the saddle was the last thing I'd be doing for a while. Reality was beginning to bite.

I was cheered a little when Jon Simmons came in. A completely different character to the stern orthopaedic surgeon, he told me not to worry; that the manner in which his colleague had delivered his diagnosis was just his way. He was the same with all the patients and I should read nothing into it.

It was exactly what I needed to hear; and from a very calm, collected plastic surgeon who has no interest in the cosmetic side of his profession whatsoever. In 2012 he treated a 28-year-old builder called Marcin Sawiki, who'd been working a circular saw on a building site in west London. Sawiki was measuring a joist and slipped, severing his hand to the point where it was hanging on by just a flap of skin. He was rushed to St Mary's in Paddington. Eight hours later Sawiki's hand had been fully reattached. An hour after that he could move his fingers. Jon took a blood vessel from his leg and grafted it onto his hand. That's a priority because there's a six-hour window that begins as soon as the blood stops flowing: with no blood supply the hand starts to die, so blood flow has to be re-established as quickly as possible. Once it had been, Jon used pins to fasten the small bones that had been severed and they were stabilised with wire. He reattached the tendons then finally the skin. Due to the quick reactions at the site, the speed of the ambulance and my surgeon's remarkable skill, that young guy still has both his hands.

As the months went on and on I'd see a lot of both Jon and Dinesh. They're brilliant surgeons and really do complement each other. Jon's role is to make sure the external wounds created by the initial accident – and the various operations thereafter – are dealt with at the same time as the orthopaedics. That way any long-term scarring and disfigurement is lessened because the soft tissue implications of the bone surgery are not an afterthought; they're taken care of there and then. It seems a natural way to work, but they tell me they're the only team in the country who operate this way.

I felt a little better after speaking to Jon, and turned my thoughts to the operations on my ankle and hand. They were going to be completed on consecutive days, and there wouldn't be much time to recover before I was due to be transferred by ambulance to Charing Cross. But I'd have friends coming in to see me all the time, and people calling on the phone. Everything was seeming much more positive…but then a couple of days later Jon examined the wound a second time and found a trace of dead skin.

Dead skin is not good, and I had to digest the possible implications as I waited to be transferred. I wasn't exactly sure what it meant so I spent the time in a balancing act, trying to absorb the facts but also trying not to dwell on it too much, keeping my mind on other things. My dad phoned to see when they were moving me and we talked about our mutual ailments – mine accidental, his down to old age. Lately he's had a problem with the nerve endings in his feet; he can no longer feel the splay of his toes which makes walking awkward. He describes it as like having no feet at all and walking on stumps. He's amazing though; he's never retired, never stopped working and at 83 has at least one more movie in him.

I remember when I finally got bored with the DT100 he'd helped me buy; something I never thought would happen when I got it. But I insisted on getting a YZ250, another two-stroke Yamaha which Dad said was way too big for me. I wasn't even 14 and everyone agreed with him – except me, so I went ahead and got it anyway. The bike arrived and Dad was right of course; it was ridiculously big for me. I could still get the front wheel up though and I'd do it time and time again as if to prove something, as if to spite him. One day he was playing tennis with a neighbour and I came racing up the dirt track I'd worn into the grass near the court. Dad was about to serve so I popped this monster wheelie just to show him I could. God, I was pleased with myself…right up until the moment I saw a stone wall looming ahead. Dropping the front wheel, I found myself in a slide I couldn't correct and the next thing I knew I was on the grass with the bike lying on top of me. Dad came over but made no move to lift it off.

'You fucking idiot,' he said. 'I told you it was too big.'

He doesn't mess around, my dad, and without that kind of approach when I was young my dyslexia would've been an even bigger issue. So little was known about the condition back then, there weren't a lot of schools that could deal with it. It was largely because of that I left St Gerard's in Ireland, and from the age of 11 I had a place as a boarder at Sibford School near Banbury.

Originally set up for the children of Quaker families, it was a really progressive place that specialised in helping people with dyslexia. I had never been away from home before though; except for when Dad was working, and that wasn't being away so much as swapping one home for another. I liked the idea of going to England and I liked the idea of being a boarder, though mostly I liked the idea of going to a school where the people who ran it didn't believe in punishment. That's how it was with the Quakers. If anyone was so far out of line that something had to be done, the headmaster would send them home, inform the parents of their behaviour and leave any punishment up to them. I thought that was fantastic, a really sensible approach to life. I've never been a saint and I realised early on that I could get away with stacks if I didn't get caught. So I was looking forward to the move, and the only fly in the ointment was being separated from Daisy. It had never really happened before; most sets of twins are very close and it was no different with the two of us.

I remember when I hadn't been there long I wrote a letter to Dad telling him that the school was alright, but I only had one friend and I didn't really think he liked me. Dad told me it broke his heart and he almost came over and fetched me. Daisy was missing me badly by then though, so he sent her to the school instead.

I grew to really love the place – we both did. The Quakers were excellent and if I'd tried a bit harder in lessons rather than dossing about and daydreaming, I might've got a couple of qualifications. As it was I stayed until I was not quite 16 and then left formal education altogether. I remember the headmaster taking me into his office that summer and wishing me well. He seemed to take some pleasure (or maybe it was just relief) in assuring me that, with my record, returning for the sixth form was not an option. I think he knew me pretty well. Anyway, a couple of years into my time there, Dad came over for a parents' day visit and asked him what I was good at. Without so much as batting an eye, he quipped: 'Not getting caught, Mr Boorman. Not getting caught.'

The only thing I initially found frustrating was that every day we'd have a period of silence. It was boring; nobody could say a word, and when you're that age sitting in silence is pure purgatory. Ironically as I got older I found that when all else fails, it's that exact kind of silence I turn to. It's my failsafe; I use silence to settle my nerves so I can formulate a plan to get out of whatever mess I find myself in.

That school was the first period in my life where I'd been settled, and after I won that solitary friend around I made lots of others. By the time I left I had received as much education as my condition would allow and I knew I wasn't going to set the world alight in the field of brain surgery or nuclear physics. I'd had bit parts in various films and I knew I ought to try and make a go of acting properly. The truth is, though, I was never that keen. I had a dream to be someone, something, but I'm not so sure it was to be an actor.

Alone in my hospital room I couldn't get away from the fear brought on by finding that dead skin. Simon came in and told me that my operations had been scheduled. He made no bones about the fact it was going to be brutal. I'd have my ankle fixed on the Monday, then on the Tuesday Mr Eckersley would work on my hand before I was moved to Charing Cross. The very next day they would get to grips with my left leg.

So we pushed ahead with the schedule; it was nil by mouth on the Sunday, then the operation on my ankle on Monday, a small window to eat – then nil by mouth again on Monday afternoon. By then though eating was quite painful anyway. During the operation to fix my ankle I was woken early from the anaesthetic because I'd vomited. They brought me round and stuffed a tube down my throat and it was really painful to swallow.

On the Tuesday I had the op on my hand, then I had to wait for them to take me to the other hospital. I'd been nervous about what was to come long before they told me about the patch of dead skin, and I kept thinking about how close I might still be to losing my leg. All that the orthopaedic surgeon had said was rattling around in my head. I needed some hope; so I phoned Ian Hutchinson.

For those of you who don't know him, Ian 'Hutchy' Hutchinson is referred to in the bike-racing world as the Miracle Man. Back in 2010, just a week after winning all five major TT races on the Isle of Man, he had the most horrific crash. He was riding for Padgett's Honda, competing in the British Supersport class at Silverstone. The track was wet and Hutchy was among a number of riders who went down on a frenetic first lap. Before he had a chance to get out of the way another bike ran over his leg.

His injuries were similar to mine with the same shattered tibia and fibula. Most riders around the paddock assumed that even if his leg was saved, his career would be over. And that would have been the case if it hadn't been for the intervention of a brilliant surgeon who happened to see his X-rays when the local surgical team was contemplating amputation.

The surgeon was Matija Krkovic, and he was pretty sure he could save the limb by performing similar surgery to what was being proposed for me. His skill and Hutchy's unbelievable will to win meant that not only did Hutchy get back on a bike, he went back to competing fiercely in road racing again. Nobody thought he had much chance of walking unaided, let alone setting new records at the Isle of Man. But he did, and with a right-hand gear shifter instead of the usual on the left. He's an inspirational figure and I'd seen him on my frequent visits to the Isle of Man after we met through the motorcycle business.

I called him up hoping for some positive feedback, but his initial response didn't allay my fears at all. When I told him what had happened and what the surgeons had talked about his reply was a little grim.

'Charley,' he said, 'that sounds pretty bad, not dissimilar to what happened to me – and it took three years and 16 operations before I was riding properly again.'

The information sent shockwaves through me. Three years. I couldn't afford three years, I had South America in September and a year from now the Darien Gap. Another cold grey cloud enveloped me and it didn't lift much when we compared X-rays over the phone. Hutchy's break was worse than mine (or at least I thought it was); the lower leg was in bits, both tibia and fibula shattered, with the breaks just above the ankle. Mine looked quite similar at first, but it was closer to my knee, which he commented on afterwards in a text.

> 'Now I've seen it, it looks a really uncomplicated break and although it's kind of smashed rather than snapped, it's in a small area so should heal well and quickly, as it's at the top of the tibia and not the bottom where blood supply is poor. Although it looks like a nice job I think the frame is the best option as, like I said, you can weight bear straight away. Let me know how you go when the frame is on and good luck.'

That message seemed to confirm that what my surgeons had mooted was the best way to go, and that encouraged me despite the fact it would be three months before they were able to say if the bone had reattached fully or not. The thought that it might not and I'd require a bone and muscle graft gnawed away at me. If the surgeons didn't see the progress they wanted to we'd be starting all over again, and I wasn't sure I could deal with that. I had to keep it real though. I had to try not to let the emotions carry me away and I told myself that if that's how it turned out, I'd just have to cope; because the alternative was to lose my leg.

When those first two operations were complete they came to take me to Charing Cross, and as I was loaded into the ambulance I spotted a guy on a Laverda Jota. An old icon from the 1970s and 80s, it reminded me of Jason's Benelli Sei. That was the first production six-cylinder motorbike ever made and he had one around the time we were in Paris. The first of what were termed 'angular' bikes, they had rectangular petrol tanks rather than the more traditional oval. The engine came from a Honda CB500 with two added cylinders and the chassis and tank were designed by Carrozzeria Ghia, a firm of bespoke Italian automobile designers that started out in Turin during World War I. Since then the company has been responsible for some truly iconic car designs, but in those early days they specialised in making lightweight aluminium bodies. Their Alpha Romeo 6C 1500 won the Mille Miglia in 1929; they followed up on that by making bodies for Fiat and Lancia. Later they designed the VW Karmann Ghia and Volvo P1800 driven by Roger Moore in *The Saint*.

The Benelli Sei was their first motorbike, and Jason rode his everywhere. Back in those days he still hadn't passed his test. It was nothing conscious or arrogant on his part, he was just really busy working as an up-and-coming young actor and somehow never quite got around to it.

Not initially, anyway. But he kept meaning to, and I remember one day in London when he was pulled over by a policeman. At first it never even occurred to him but then, as the officer approached, it started to dawn on him; he tried to work out what he could say to get him out of the hole. He was about to come clean and apologise, admit his mistake without waiting to be asked – but the copper only wanted a closer look at the red-and-chrome monster he was riding. He told Jason he was a biker himself and had never seen anything like it, and to get in touch if he ever wanted to sell. He wrote down his name and phone number, and, as it turned out, that's exactly what Jason did a few months later.

He's long since passed his test of course; that was way back in the early 1980s when we were flitting between London and Paris. My speech had improved dramatically and I wasn't stuttering as much as I had been, my confidence having been rebuilt by the efforts of the school. I was more into motorbikes than ever and I was jealous of Jason's Sei.

It was a few years after I'd left school; I did a whole bunch of different movies, then I went to Paris to be close to my oldest sister, Telsche, who was like a second mother to me. She had been living over there for a while, having stayed on after she and Katrine completed a Cordon Bleu culinary course at the Sorbonne. They both spoke fluent French, and since Telsche was living with her boyfriend Arnaud Sélignac, an up-and-coming director, it was clear that France was where my sister was making her home.

Dad then got involved in the production of a 1984 film called *Nemo*, which Arnaud directed, and subsequently bought a small apartment not far from where Telsche was living. It was a short, wonderful period where we were all together because Katrine was also appearing in *Nemo* and I had a tiny part too. It was a brilliant time; we were in a great business and we were all young and ambitious. While I was out there I used Dad's flat as a base before I hooked up again with Jason. We'd known each other on and off since those days on the monkey bike a decade earlier, but it was during those few months in Paris where our friendship really started to flourish.

All my biking was still off-road, though I'd got rid of that YZ250 everyone said was too big. I remember taking a sensible step backwards to a much more manageable 125 and then a Suzuki. I was just about old enough to take my test and I wanted to get it out of the way so I didn't get caught out like Jason almost had. I didn't have the money for a new bike but something second-hand would do. Jason had more money than I did, being three years older and already a successful actor; he also had a decent role in *Nemo*. It's a good little movie where a young boy imagines being in a story he is yet to hear, encountering all manner of weird and wonderful beings as well as famous characters from history. Jason played Nemo as a teenager and I, well, I had this massively important pivotal role as the elevator operator. Not a huge part, I'll grant you, no BAFTAs or Oscars; but at least I wasn't merely listed as 'elevator operator'. I was an elevator operator called Cunegond.

When I first got to Paris, as I mentioned, I stayed in the flat my dad had bought close to where Telsche lived. It was small and crowded though, so pretty soon I graduated to sharing with Jason. Dad finished the work he was doing on *Nemo* and by then he was well into the planning stage of *The Emerald Forest*. Unbeknown to me at the time he had earmarked me for the leading role as Tomme, a teenage boy found by his father ten years after he was abducted by a tribe of Amazonian Indians.

That film was one of the first real environmentally conscious movies, a dramatic human story about a six-year-old taken by a tribe whose lands were being eroded by deforestation. Without any darker purpose in mind, on seeing the young boy they thought he would be better with their way of life rather than that of his father, whose company was cutting down the trees they depended on for their survival. The film was way ahead of its time and, as I said, Dad wanted me in it from the get-go. Whoever played Tomme would have to do their own stunts and he knew he could trust me to do that. He also knew this was a real opportunity for me to use all my experience and make a name for myself, a chance to fully restore the confidence I'd lost when I started to try to read.

The studio was dead against the idea of giving me the part, but then my dad has fought with studios all his life. Producers and financiers can be the bane of a director's existence. Dad's renowned in the industry for taking on really tough assignments and I'm sure some of that desire to push boundaries has rubbed off on me. He asked the studio why he shouldn't use his son, who was more than capable of playing the role, and they never really gave him a reason. Production was held up for a couple of weeks with the whole thing creating a bit of a rumpus. There were lots of meetings and phone calls, huge arguments about who should play the role of this boy missing in the Amazon rainforest.

In the end Dad called their bluff. He screen-tested two other actors for the part as well as me and sent all three tests back to Hollywood. He didn't state who the actors were, just told the producers to look at the tests and make their choice. They did, and the verdict was unanimous: they wanted the blue-eyed blond-haired kid to wear the paint and loincloth.

I have to say, it was pretty weird being the subject of so much argument and conjecture. In truth, I'd never really wanted the role because I was the victim of nepotism comments as much on the set as anywhere else. A film set can be a pretty daunting place with not only the rest of the cast watching your every move, but also the crew. All of them are professionals and expect the same level of expertise from everyone. There I was, John Boorman's son, with hardly any credits to my own name, and I'd have to carry many scenes by myself. I had to be persuaded, coerced and cajoled and it was only the promise of a dirt bike to ride while off set that made me agree to do it. I was young and naïve enough to believe it would be forthcoming, but in reality there was no way the insurance company would've had it. That didn't stop me pestering my dad, though.

'Where's the motorbike?' I would ask him. 'We've got a few days off from filming, Dad, where's the dirt bike you promised me?' It didn't show up of course, but the film and my role in it was a great success. I went back to Paris as a bona fide actor with my confidence restored and a serious credit to my name. Jason will tell you – it was a very different Charley that hooked up with him again.

We had some great times back then and many of them took place in the flat Jason and I shared, which was on the floor above an apartment owned by a great friend of Telsche's. It was a guy called Philip Esteppe, an American living the life in Paris; he'd made a stack of money as a hedge-funder or something on Wall Street. Compared to the two of us he was pretty civilised – how he lived, I mean, cleanliness and what have you. One day he came up to our place and when he stepped inside he literally gagged. Hand to his nose he said, 'Jesus, what's that godawful smell?'

I seem to remember Jason and I were only just recovering from the night before, and we looked at each other with no clue what he was talking about.

'The stench,' Philip said. 'Can't you smell it? It's horrendous, really; it's enough to make you throw up.'

We took a look around to see if we could figure out what he meant and where such a smell might be coming from. It took a moment or two before I noticed a pile of dishes left over from the dinner party we'd had the second night we'd moved in. I tried to work out when that was and started counting the days. When I ran out of fingers I realised enough had passed for a layer of green mould to grow on some of the dirtier dishes.

'Oh, that smell,' I said. 'Right, the washing up. Yeah, I've been meaning to get to it.'

PART THREE

12 – 17 March 2016:
Charing Cross Hospital,
London, England

FEARLESS (OR TRYING TO BE)

As soon as I was settled in my room at Charing Cross, Jon Simmons the plastic surgeon took another good look at my leg. I'd already had a plethora of X-rays and CT scans and there were black-and-white images on computer screens everywhere I looked. With a slight hint of teeth-sucking, he told me it was what he called 'a nasty comminuted proximal tibial fracture' but stopped short of telling me I was lucky to still have the leg. I was glad about that. I was tired of hearing it, though it would arise again and again during the coming months and from various different doctors.

We talked about the upcoming operation, my third in as many days, and he explained that the wounds should be closed by the end of the procedure. There was a small chance they would not, but it would depend on what was found when they opened my leg. He said it might be that I'd need some more soft tissue work and in that case the wound would have to remain open. He also said they'd be sampling the fracture site for any bacteria, given the patch of dead skin. That might have some impact on my long-term prognosis. He didn't elaborate, but I knew what he was talking about.

The next day an orderly came up to my room and wheeled me down to theatre. What's good about that is the fact that you're still in your own bed, which goes a long way to allay the potential for panic. You leave the room in the bed you've been sleeping in, and when you wake up after theatre you're still in that same bed. That said, I was nervous and emotional. Both Olly and Katrine were in the room and as the orderly took me down I had to fight to stop from breaking down completely.

By now I just wanted to get it over with. Three in three days – I was pretty beaten up and the anaesthetist could see that. Mixing up ingredients in what he called a 'chemical piña colada', he was a bit of a biker so we had quite a chat before he slipped in the needle. Lying with my head to one side I could see through the open doors into theatre, and it looked like a modern-day version of Frankenstein's laboratory. All that the orthopaedic surgeon had said about limb salvation, bone and muscle grafts, blood supply and infection – it all came whirling back. I could see what I thought was a bone saw and that just about finished me so I told him to go ahead and put me under.

In what seemed no time at all I woke to the most horrific pain. Really, I'm not kidding – there's pain and there's pain, and I'd felt a lot of it quite recently, but that seemed like absolutely nothing to me now. This was unbelievable; way worse than what I'd suffered at the roadside. I reached down to grab my knee and saw this space-age looking frame encircling the lower half of my leg. It gave me a hell of a shock, all pins and metal bars, bolts and tensioners, spools of wire poking into the flesh of my leg. Where they'd taken the metal plate out there was a piece of plastic linked to a tube that ran down to a box on the floor that was acting like a hoover to suck up all the blood and gunge.

The sight of all that seemed to add to the pain and it was so intense I was gasping, sweating; I wanted to throw up. My throat felt like I'd swallowed a bowl of thorns – it was so scratched from all the tubes that had been shoved down it over the past few days. I was ridiculously thirsty, my tongue so swollen it seemed to fill my mouth. But the pain took away all other thoughts. The nurse gave me morphine, but it didn't make any difference. She gave me some more and it had no effect at all. She was really stressed by now and in the end she phoned the surgeons. They came into the recovery room and took a look, but all seemed as it should be from a surgical point of view. Yet somehow I was still in agony. As I sat up again I noticed that the bottom half of my foot was twisted ever so slightly. It was putting pressure on my knee, and that's where the pain was coming from. Reaching down I managed to straighten the foot and the horrific pain subsided.

The relief was incredible. I was able to lie back so the nurse could give me some water to drink; just small sips initially but enough to take away the thirst that was almost as bad as the pain. She showed me how the morphine drip worked – a little button on the tube with a light attached, that was linked to a bag on one of those roll-along pulleys. She said that whenever that light came on I could press the button and get a shot. From that moment on I just watched for the light and as soon as it was illuminated I jabbed the button.

That night I was absolutely exhausted. I think I had something to eat then I fell asleep and had the weirdest dreams, probably because of the morphine. I remember a sensation where my whole body was in spasm and I felt that I was literally sinking into the bed. It was like I was drowning, and no matter what I did I couldn't escape the sea of blankets.

In the morning, Dinesh the bone surgeon came in to see me and explained that when they had opened the wound they'd seen first-hand that the 'comminution' was pretty significant. (I looked that word up later and it means the reduction of a solid material from one average size to a smaller average size, and in this case the solid material was the proximal third of my tibia.) They told me the fracture had remained unstable despite the plate so they'd taken it out and fitted the frame. It's like a cage that surrounds your leg, effectively moving the weight-bearing aspect from the shattered section of bone to the external frame. Once the plate had been removed they pieced all the fragments together as best they could then stitched the wound. The frame allows the bone to regrow, taking your weight off the bone and the wound itself so you are able to get around on crutches while recovering. That's the theory anyway; but it helps if your other ankle isn't broken and pinned as mine was. It meant I'd be wheelchair-bound for six or eight weeks.

That was really depressing; hearing it was one of the lowest points since I found myself lying among all that motorcycle debris. I came out of theatre with the frame on my leg and they sent off samples of tissue to see what was happening in terms of the dreaded infection.

As if he sensed just when I needed him, Jason called from Scotland, and I sucked up the conversation like a thirsty man at a well. I needed to keep my mind busy, to stop fixating on what could go wrong with my leg. There was nothing I could do physically but I think the input from friends in those early days kept me from feeling any sorrier for myself.

I was in constant pain, and it wasn't just my leg and ankle – my face was aching down one side. Probably where the muscles had been stretched by the plethora of tubes stuck down my throat, it was a weird sensation that reminded me of a night with Jason in Paris as we walked down the Rue St Denis. I'd had a couple of glasses of wine and was staring at this stunningly beautiful young woman on the street peddling her wares among the other girls. I remember wondering what on earth someone like that was doing working the streets and the next thing I knew, I walked right into a lamp post. I went down as if poleaxed. Everyone around me was laughing – everyone except Jason, who was walking away as if he had no idea who I was. I yelled out to him, 'Jason! Jason! Wait up!' Nothing; nonchalant as you like, he just carried on.

Despite that, we came back to London a year later with a bond that's remained unbroken. I found a place to live and thought about being a courier between acting jobs, but knew I'd never be any good because I'd always get the addresses mixed up. I had to pass my bike test first anyway, but the thought of screwing up addresses brought back my inability with the written word and that seemed to undermine my newfound confidence. The issues I'd had as a child had filtered into every area of my life and that included acting. If I was going to make it I had to be able to learn lines for auditions, and I knew that would be a nightmare. I don't mind admitting that I was really freaked out by the idea of being in front of a casting director and stumbling over lines I hadn't been able to memorise. I knew I would stutter and stammer and that would bring back the pain of those early days in Annamoe, trying to read with my dad.

Somehow I knew I had to deal with it. If I was going to capitalise on what I'd achieved with *The Emerald Forest* I had no choice. I tried not to think too much about it though, and instead of going to auditions I set about making sure I passed my bike test. I still coveted Jason's Benelli; it was a hell of a bike despite the usual electrical problems that come with any Italian machine, and he used to grind the footpegs when taking corners. He got bored though, and sold it to that policeman.

Jason had way more money than I did and I remember that after he sold the Benelli he bought himself a Yamaha Super Ténéré: a forerunner to the BMW R1150GS that Ewan and I rode around the world. The Ténéré came on the market in 1989 with two models, the XTZ 660 and XTZ 750, both of which were way ahead of their time in terms of being an on road/off road adventurer. They were reminiscent of the BMWs in that they were taller than a road bike, and the suspension was designed to cope with more than just the tarmac. The 660 was a single cylinder and the 750 a twin. Both engines contained five-valve heads and the 750 won the Dakar Rally twice in its original form then four more times after it had been upgraded to an 850.

Looking back at those bikes now, and seeing how so many people are riding the modern-day versions, it's obvious that biking has evolved from either road or off-road to a mishmash of both. After the Ténéré Jason moved onto a Kawasaki GPZ900R, a real beast of a bike by anyone's standards, and I was even more envious. When I think about it, he was something of a serial buyer and seller. He did a lot of exchanging of both bikes and cars and lost a lot of money in the process. He'd buy something but only keep it for a matter of weeks before he was onto the next.

Back then Jason and I spent a huge amount of time together – and not just in London and Paris, but Los Angeles as well. I remember one Sunday when we were riding Honda 250 motocrossers in this specially designed off-road park up in the Sierras, with Francesco Quinn. It was 80 square miles spliced with off-road tracks that had been worn deep into the hillside by decades of use. People would come out in their Winnebago motorhomes with motorbikes strapped on the back and spend the weekend dirt-tracking.

That place wasn't far from Francesco's house and he was as much into motorbikes as Jason and I were. He was the son of American actor Anthony Quinn, and one of ten brothers and sisters. Francesco's mother was Iolanda Addolori, Anthony's second wife. He and Jason did a film together in 1989 called *Casablanca Express* about a plot to kill Winston Churchill, but he got his break playing Rhah in *Platoon* in 1986. He was a super-fit guy and great fun. In a tragic irony he died from a massive heart attack while running up the road with his son.

I remember Francesco being the greatest of blaggers; the kind of person who always seemed to get free this and free that from all manner of unlikely sources. We'd go to his house and it was always full of the latest gadgets. We used to tell him that he managed to live a champagne lifestyle on what amounted to beer money. He seemed to have various deals going with different motorcycle companies, and his garage was an Aladdin's cave of delicious goodies. He had a bespoke Ducati Monster, and various bikes from a deal with Honda where they'd give him a new one every three months. The garage was littered with all the different makes and models and he was very good on all of them. He was pretty blasé about it though, and whenever we asked how he came by so many bikes he'd just laugh it off and tell us it was easy to make deals for motorbikes. Basically, he would promote either the brand or the dealer by being seen around LA on their machines. I think subconsciously I absorbed that. To some extent I've put it into practice myself with various companies, most notably BMW and, of course, Triumph. I've made motorbikes my sole source of income in one form or another and even with my leg as it was I was determined to keep it that way.

Within a few days of that second operation on my left leg I was back in theatre for a third. When the surgeons opened me up to assess what the Portuguese had done they'd been concerned about one particular piece of bone. With the frame in place they'd taken another look via X-ray and decided it was floating too freely and was therefore unlikely to fuse on its own. There was a chance it might die, and we could not afford that – so they inserted an additional pin at the top of the frame to hold the fragment in place in the hope it would fuse and begin to regrow.

When I came to after that operation the surgeon told me it had gone well. As a precaution he was prescribing an anticoagulant called Apixaban and was going to give me plenty of antibiotics which I would administer myself if there was any sign of infection. He also recommended using an Exogen machine which uses ultrasound to augment the bone healing.

Back in my room Daisy was waiting. She still lives in Fulham, on the same street where Olly and I lived for years with our daughters. We moved to Barnes six years ago and, apart from low-flying aircraft en route to Heathrow, it has a real village feel though it's right in the loop of the Thames. I told Daisy I was sick of being laid up in hospital and itching to get home. I knew I'd still be laid up when I got there, of course; I'd be that way for months. But at least I would be at home and for the sake of my sanity it was vital to get back to some semblance of normality. Daisy told me I had to be patient – but I'm never patient, I never have been.

I've been this way all my life. If I see something new I want to try it, be it riding a horse or a motorbike or driving a car. I remember when we were about 10 or 11 Daisy and I were dossing about in Dad's car. He'd left the keys in the ignition and it was an automatic; we got the engine started and the car in gear. Between us we worked out that controlling a car wasn't that hard and made it all the way to the end of the drive. Now we had to turn around and the only way to do that was to back up. I found reverse and trundled along the drive again to the only place we could turn. By now my sister was itching to get her hands on the wheel and was doing everything she could to wrench it out of my hands. She was tugging one way and I the other and the car started to slide. With both of us trying to steer we were too far over on the slope and, slowly, inexorably we headed for the neighbouring ditch. Before we knew it we were past the point of no return and ended up with the car on its side. We were panicking, sure it would completely tip over. Somehow it didn't, but we had to climb out through the driver's window, and still faced the prospect of telling Dad. It was a big, fairly expensive car and it took us ages to pluck up the courage to walk back to the house. Eventually we did – and I can't remember which one of us actually told him. He stood there for a moment; then he just shrugged his shoulders and phoned a neighbour with a tractor to pull it out.

Dad's not fazed by that kind of thing. Possessions have never been important to him; a car was just a car and all he was concerned about was the fact nobody got hurt. I remember another time in Mum's taxi. It was one of the old London black cabs from the 1970s that she drove as her car in Ireland. I was younger then; the only way I could see through the windscreen was to stand on the seat. Dad was in the living room in a meeting with some important people about a movie. The room looks over the drive and he was in mid-flow when suddenly he stopped. He could see Mum's cab crawling down the slope with me standing on the seat at the steering wheel. Dashing outside he made a run for the door to stop me crashing – but by then I was in the rhododendron bush.

Daisy was right, of course; I had to be patient, but I was desperate. The last time I'd seen my house had been almost a month ago. Winter was turning to spring and I wanted to be among familiar surroundings. My only means of getting around would be a wheelchair, and it would be different but at least I would be at home. It was such a pity I'd broken my other ankle. When they fitted Hutchy with the spatial frame he was up on crutches straight away, gradually increasing the weight on his injured leg. He was in the gym, he was swimming, he was exercising on a fixed bicycle. That wasn't going to happen with me. I couldn't put any weight on my left leg until my other ankle was fully mended and I could use it to support me. Even then the maximum the surgeons would allow me was 20 per cent of my body weight. That meant no stairs of course, and our bedroom is on the second floor. One flight was one too many, let alone two, so for the time being at least it would have to be a bed downstairs.

Daisy stayed for a while and tried to take my mind off my leg by talking about the days we'd spent together at Sibford School. She was a much better student than I was; much more focused and accomplished in the classroom, and also a great all-round sportswoman. (I remember one awards ceremony when she was called to the stage for the umpteenth time and I was in the front row in full view of her with a hand to my mouth, mid-yawn.)

She took off and I called Olivia at the house where Richard and Roy, two of my oldest friends, were organising my life for the foreseeable future. They had set up a bed downstairs – hearing that, I was even more desperate to get out of the hospital. There was nothing to do here. I had too much time to think; though I don't know why I was under the impression it would be any different at home. I would still be on my back. I'd still have a pee bottle and a bedpan. It was all a little depressing and that date three months from now remained at the back of my mind: D-Day, when I'd find out if the frame that encompassed my leg had worked or if I was staring down the barrel of more operations.

I fixed that date as the critical juncture I had to get to. But there were other waypoints, markers in my road book to recovery. That's how I began to think of it; a rally, a journey, an expedition marked on a map like the rolling road book I was issued with when I raced the Dakar. I'd ridden the long way round and the long way down and now I was attempting to make the long way back. The first waypoint was the wheelchair here at the hospital, the second going home. The third was moving from bedpan to commode and maybe, dare I dream about the possibility, the commode to an actual toilet. After that it would be each individual consultation, then D-Day, South America in September and, all being well, the finish line: the Darien Gap.

All just fine in principle but everything rested on that consultation in June and it hung like the sword of Damocles above me. I hated the idea of beginning again. Taking bone from my hip would be painful and involve muscle from my calf being brought around to my shin so the graft would have its own independent blood supply. I had my livelihood to think about. Already I'd missed the Australian tour and my duties with Triumph had been curtailed dramatically. I still had to earn some money and I was hoping that even if I couldn't ride in South America come September, I'd at least be fit enough to travel in the support vehicle. I was hopeful. September still felt a long way off, but when you're lying in a hospital bed with a cast on your right leg and a futuristic-looking cage on your left, you feel so helpless that nothing really seems possible.

I was slipping again emotionally. I remember talking to Kinvara, my youngest daughter, who was about to go off to university. The day I had the accident she was halfway through a ski season in the French Alps. Working as a chalet host, her hours were early morning and evening as she cooked and cleaned for guests as part of her gap year.

She was off duty and having a burger with friends when she received a text from Olly telling her I'd been involved in an accident. She'd immediately tried to FaceTime me on her phone, but it wasn't me that answered – it was Nigel from Triumph. The unexpected face sent Kinvara into a blind panic.

'Where's my dad?' she said.

'He's not here, you can't talk to him right now.'

'Why not? Where is he? Who are you?'

'My name's Nigel, I work for Triumph and I was with your dad when he had the accident.'

'Did you see what happened?'

'No, not exactly. I arrived just a bit after. He can't talk to you, Kinvara; he's having an operation.'

Now Kinvara really started to panic. 'Operation?' she said. 'What kind of operation? Is he going to be OK?'

'He'll be fine,' Nigel assured her. 'I can't really tell you much more til he comes out of theatre, but I'm sure he's going to be fine.'

When I finally got to speak to her she told me she'd left the restaurant and gone downstairs where she would have some privacy. After talking to Nigel, though, she felt as if she was just left hanging. When she went back up to the restaurant her friends had hidden what remained of her hamburger and thought it hugely funny. A prank, a joke, but to Kinvara at that moment it seemed such a stupid a thing to do and she burst into floods of tears.

With my hopes of going home seeming more realistic now, I was getting used to the frame on my leg. The pins were a little uncomfortable, there was a bloody great dent in my shin where the bone should be and the flesh was permanently swollen. That was all normal apparently, but I was always concerned about the risk of infection. My surgeon made a point of telling me that the threat to my leg would remain until the bone had fully regrown and my recovery was complete. To do otherwise would've been remiss, but it began to invade my dreams. In the hospital, particularly, I had nightmares. The one I mentioned before, my morphine-induced panic about sinking into the bed and drowning, kept returning again and again.

I was still hopeful that a 'complete recovery' would be sooner rather than later, though there had been talk of more than a year. I'm not religious but I was nigh-on praying that when the X-rays were done in June everything would be as it should be. Meanwhile I had familiar surroundings to look forward to; but that meant being in a wheelchair, and the nurses were keen for me to get used to it.

I didn't want to get in the chair. I didn't want to move at all. To move was really uncomfortable because I couldn't put any weight on my feet, other than on my left heel to use it as a pivot. Moving meant swinging from one sitting position to another with my legs dangling at least for a couple of seconds. Dangling limbs carry all their weight and that was incredibly painful, particularly where the pins and bolts of the frame entered my flesh. It was also really awkward; the frame was there to enable me to bear weight gradually and it wasn't that cumbersome when I was upright. But with a broken and dislocated right ankle I couldn't actually be upright, so I was constantly having to change position where the frame rested on a cushion propped up on the bed.

During those last few days in hospital I was in and out of the wheelchair, getting used to seeing the world from a very different perspective. It really wasn't easy, and it's left me in awe of the way that permanently disabled people adapt. I'm a two-wheel man and the last time I'd been mobile had been on a Triumph, popping the occasional wheelie. Now I was on four wheels needing someone to push me around, though I convinced myself it was only temporary. (As my recovery continued I'd be able to wheel myself down into town for coffee and whatnot, but in those early days I wasn't able to do anything under my own steam.) I was wheeled along the corridors with the sights and sounds of the hospital all around me, one leg bandaged on a foot rest and the other horizontal and sticking out in front of me.

The first time Olly pushed me along the hospital corridor I had the morphine bag suspended on a wheeled pulley at the back of the chair. It was attached to a tube that attached to me, the one with the button I mentioned earlier. At the same time I still had the plastic cover on my leg, the suction pump that fed the waste basin and the tubes gathered in my lap. Olly was wheeling me over to the nurses' station to take a look at some X-rays and as we turned away to go back to my room, the tube from the vacuum got caught in the wheel. The whole thing went crashing down – the basin with all the crap from my leg, the stand for the morphine – it slapped the floor so hard that the bag of liquid burst. There was morphine all over the place and nothing when I pressed the button, no pain relief; for a second I was in a blind panic.

Olly looked at me and the mess we'd made and shook her head. 'God,' she said, 'all we did was come a few yards. We haven't even tried to leave the hospital yet.'

ECHOES OF THE PAST

Was this the shape of things to come? I hoped not. Back in my room I took a call from Roy to tell me that he and Richard had got the bed set up and everything was ready at home. He also told me he planned to check the lock-up where we both keep a couple of bikes. The last time I'd been down there I noticed some rust on my bobber and mentioned it to him. It was a little damper in the shed than we'd thought and I was concerned about that bike going to rat shit.

Roy and I go way back – friends since my late teens when he helped me locate my very first road bike. It was a Kawasaki Zephyr 750 that I bought not long after I got back from Paris. They look a little dated now but they'd been styled on the iconic Z1 which Kawasaki built between 1972 and 1975. The Z1 was the sort of versatile upright road bike they call a 'standard', a muscle bike that prioritised power, and there was a gap of more than 15 years between the last Z1 they manufactured and the first of the Zephyrs. Kawasaki made them as 400s for the Japanese market, then a 550, 750 and 1100 for the rest of the world. I loved that bike. I treasured it, and it's the only machine I've ever actually made money on.

Back then Roy ran one of the coolest bike shops in London. Bullet Motorcycles on the New King's Road stocked the best range of clothing and helmets you could get at the time. He made a point of pasting 'Bullet' stickers wherever he could, on every bike he sold as well as every helmet – you still see them all over London. It wasn't just biker stuff; it was streetwear heavily influenced by the surfer/biker crossover scene in California. In many ways, it was similar to the custom crossover store Deus Ex Machina in Australia, though Roy's shop was on a much smaller scale. He had this massive chair where you could take your time to flip through bike magazines and catalogues of gear and apparel. The chair was so enormous that, cartoon-like, it enveloped a man so he looked no bigger than a child. Quirky, imaginative, the whole place bore the stamp of Roy's personality. He didn't have a bike he could sell me then, but knew of a grey import Zephyr on the other side of town.

He took me there on the back of his bike – and I hate riding pillion (show me a biker who doesn't). We took off late and knew the shop would be closing, so he rode as fast as he could. I was amazed and terrified at the speed with which he bobbed through traffic. He would cut between buses and cabs, zip over crossroads, switch lanes between the vehicles and make red lights just before they changed from amber. Most of my riding had been off-road; I was only just

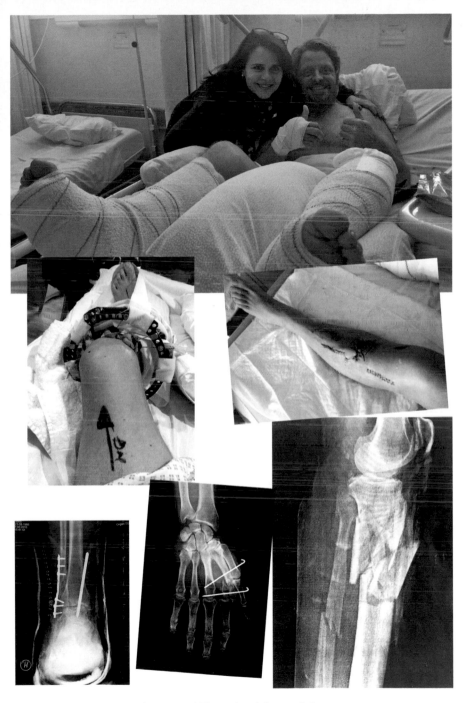

Ana, my roadside angel, and the mess below

Dad on the set of *Point Blank* with Lee and Angie

TOP: Dad on the set of *Deliverance* with Burt Reynolds, Jon Voight and Ned Beatty;
MIDDLE: Mum with Burt behind the scenes of *Deliverance*;
BOTTOM: My groovy mum with Telsche and Katrine in Malibu

CLOCKWISE FROM TOP: Daisy with Lee; Daisy and me with the wonderful Mrs Miller; My first tux; Daisy and me with Telsche and Katrine, who were always dressing us up; Mum and Dad with Daisy and me during the *Hell in the Pacific* shoot

Top: Looking cool in South Carolina; **Main:** Dad and me in Ireland;
Bottom: With Daisy in Malibu

TOP INSET: Dad and me at Cape Agulhas, South Africa;
MIDDLE INSET: Flying the Cessna in South Africa;
MAIN AND BOTTOM: Family photos at home in Ireland

TOP LEFT: Jason Connery and me in Paris; **TOP RIGHT:** Daisy and me with my beloved Yamaha;
MIDDLE: In Brazil shooting *The Emerald Forest*;
BOTTOM: Dinner with friends whilst promoting *The Emerald Forest* in LA with Powers Boothe

TOP: My 21st at the Groucho Club in London with Olly;
MIDDLE: Track day on a Suzuki GSX–R750 SRAD; **BOTTOM:** Generace and the team

MAIN: Life before *Long Way Round*;
INSET: My godson Sam and me on my first proper road bike, a Kawasaki Zephyr 750

Top: 5-up on my Yamaha DT-100 – Kinvara, Lee, myself, Doone and Lola;
Main: Sat on my '59 Triumph from The Baron's Speed Shop with Dad in Ireland

MAIN: My girls and me in the ancient oak forest where we shot *Excalibur*;
BOTTOM: Mum and Dad with the girls

The *Long Way Round* – Ewan and myself, with guest appearances from
Dave, Russ and the Road of Bones

The *Long Way Down*, featuring my girls and (**BOTTOM LEFT**) the great Claudio von Planta

Clockwise from top left: My *The Wild Ones* tribute bike, beautifully worked by Hawg Haven; Can you guess which one is Ross Noble?; Some of my bikes; Promo shoot for Movember; My gorgeous Ziggy

CLOCKWISE FROM TOP LEFT: *By Any Means* in Papua New Guinea; My great friend Roy, who sold me my first proper road bike; Billy and me on one of our motorcycle tours in Africa; The pain of Dakar (© Hans–Peter van Velthoven)

CLOCKWISE FROM TOP LEFT: My beautiful sister Telsche – we miss you;
Ross Noble and me at Fish River Canyon, Namibia; Kinvara's 18th birthday;
Messing around on a private road in Sydney!; Daisy and my beloved mother

back from Paris and that was my first real experience of beating the traffic in London.

Riding a motorbike is all about confidence – the more confident you are, the better you ride – and I suppose that applies to most ventures in life. It's no truer than when riding the streets of London though, as any hesitation is dangerous. I remember Roy taking this one set of crossroads where we were so close to getting clipped by a bus that I shut my eyes. Stomach in my mouth, I waited for the collision – but, thankfully, it never came.

Miraculously we just about managed to get there in one piece, the shop hadn't closed, and there was the Zephyr. I thought it was absolutely gorgeous. Roy knew much more about what to look for in a second-hand bike than I did and checked it over for me. I'd offered to pay him to do that, but he told me there was no need. He reckoned it was pretty clean so I bought it, and soon afterwards I was carving up traffic on the streets of the city like the veteran courier I'd never managed to be.

It really was a good piece of kit, every bit as usable as its predecessors; comfortable to ride and planted considering it was effectively a naked superbike. It was air-cooled with twin shock rear suspension. The 1100 was a little different, incorporating aspects of the GPZ1100 and the old Z1000. That bike had two spark plugs per cylinder whereas all the other Zephyr models had just one. Back in Ireland, my neighbour Kaz heard I'd got the 750 so, of course, he went out and bought the 1100. Bigger and better as always, he didn't stop there; no sooner had he taken delivery then the bike was off to the local Harris outfitters for all the extras he could get. They've been building race chassis, exhausts, carbs and more for almost as long as motorbikes have been raced. But I didn't care. The 750 was more suited to London than a big old 1100 and this was my first real road bike. My bike is long since gone, but the one Kaz owned is still being ridden by another great mate of mine, Angus Jones.

I kept the Zephyr for a long time and when I did eventually sell it, it was for a Suzuki GSX-R750 similar to what Chris Walker used to ride in the British Superbike series. I remember seeing him on a track day at Brands Hatch not long after I first met Ewan. During the 1990s I was a track day junkie, regularly riding Donington, Brands, Mallory Park, negotiating the Bomb Hole at Snetterton. Ewan and I used to do loads of track days together and ended up fronting a racing team in British Superstock. That day at Brands though I was riding really well, into my umpteenth lap, coming up to the hairpin and my braking marker and feeling like a natural-born racer. Chris Vermeulen, the Australian Moto GP star, once told me that racing is simple – if you're not accelerating or braking you're wasting time.

It had been a particularly satisfying day, and as I was coming to the hairpin I took two other riders on the brakes – meaning I was braking later than they were, so when they were starting to slow down I was yet to grab the lever. I remember thinking it was the best bit of track riding I'd ever done, that nobody could've braked later than I did. Or so I thought. As I came to the marker that indicated my point to start braking, another GSX-R750 was suddenly alongside me. The rider was changing up a gear. I could not believe it. I could've sworn to God you couldn't brake any later than I did, and there's this guy still accelerating. I was so gobsmacked I almost crashed as he put the bike into a two-wheel drift, squared off the hairpin and took off. I'd never seen riding like it, and as he hunched over the tank I recognised the distinctive riding style and realised it was Chris Walker. I'd seen him on a few track days before, either testing or just keeping his hand in. He's very popular around the circuit even now; a self-effacing little guy from Nottingham who lost the British Superbike Championship to Neil Hodgson after his bike broke down, when he sat by the fence and sobbed.

Back at the hospital I was as far from a racetrack as I'd ever been; but at least I was going home. The morning Olly came to fetch me, I climbed from my bed – hopefully for the last time – plonked into the wheelchair, and the nurses took me in the lift to the ground floor.

My wife was waiting with our dog Ziggy in the Nissan Micra we'd bought for Doone and Kinvara. Costing £1,000, we'd found it at the back of a forecourt, hidden away behind shiny MINI Convertibles and VW Golfs. For a long time during my recovery it was the only car I could get in and out of because it's two-door and everything is at the right level. It was ironic because I had a brand new Range Rover sitting outside my house that they'd supplied me with as part of my role as a company ambassador.

I've been involved with them for a while; they make the best off-road vehicles around and it was a Range Rover that sparked my interest in the Darien Gap. Years ago, I read the account of a crossing made by the explorer Colonel John Blashford-Snell. That was back in 1972 and he accomplished it in a Range Rover. A dozen years before, though, it was a Land Rover named *La Cucaracha Cariñosa* ('The Affectionate Cockroach') that made the first vehicular crossing of the Gap. It was driven by Amado and Reina Arauz from Panama and accompanied by a Jeep carrying an ex-SAS trooper and an Australian engineer. They set out from Chepo in Panama on 2 February 1960 and reached Quibdo, Colombia on 17 June. It took 136 days to make the crossing and they'd averaged a distance of 200 yards per hour.

That's how tough the Gap is and it was my goal for recovery, the finish line I was aiming for. But that was a long way off – first, I had to walk again. I was finally home though, which was another small step along the way. I had a single bed set up in the conservatory, so I could see both the garden and the 60-inch TV I'd just bought which would keep me occupied for at least some of the time.

Olivia had spent £300 on a wheelchair, but we also had to buy a commode. It was effectively another wheelchair but with a toilet seat and bucket underneath. Every morning for the next couple of months, my long-suffering wife's first job would be to remove the bucket and get rid of the waste, then scrub it with bleach. Up until that moment I'd been using bedpans and I had a pee bottle along with the TV remote on the cabinet she'd placed by the bed. Next to that was the commode and a small green chair that I used as a link between the two, where I could pivot on my heels while I slung myself from the chair to the commode or the commode back to the chair. One time when I was en route, the chair slid away and my foot hit the floor so hard that my knee rocked forward with my foot on the floor and the lower part of my leg right back underneath me. For a moment, I just stared. I cannot tell you what was going through my mind. I was sweating, panicking; the doctors had told me not to let my leg bend more than 90 degrees because the tendon that overlaid the kneecap might snap.

Thankfully it seemed to be OK, and I worked myself back into the chair again. It was during moments like those that I really understood how incapacitated I actually was. I'd been like it for a month already but all that time I'd been in hospital with people coming and going. Nurses, orderlies, cleaners and caterers were on hand; if I needed anything all I had to do was press a button and somebody would come in to help.

Now it was just Olly and me. The morphine was gone, no more intravenous painkillers — I was taking paracetamol every four hours. It's a tip I'd been given by Hutchy to keep the pain at bay and one that was echoed by my doctors. I had a good supply of the antibiotics my surgeon had prescribed and I'd been told to keep a close eye on the pins where they protruded from the skin. Any pus had to be cleared right away, and I needed to watch for excessive redness in the skin and anything that felt more tender than what I was used to. I couldn't take ibuprofen as it inhibits bone growth. I'd had a few infections around the pin sites already but I took the drugs and tried not to worry. Pus would gather and congeal and I had to pick it away then swab the area with disinfectant. I know it sounds gross – and it is gross – but those pins were the focus of my attention and would remain so for months.

Now I was home the lack of assistance was apparent and I was learning to deal with all sorts of new situations. Sometimes I was home alone; the girls were away and Olly had stuff to do. Much as I tried to plan for when she was out, I'm absentminded at the best of times and one morning she went into town leaving me with a cup of tea and my pee bottle. That was fine, but I hadn't realised that the bottle was just out of reach. As it turned out the commode was also just out of reach and, of course, I needed to pee.

I was lying there thinking there was no way I'd be able to hold on until Olly got home, and trying to work out what I could do. Suddenly I noticed my mug of tea. I drained it, then hunched up in the bed and held the empty mug at an angle where I hoped it wouldn't spill. It was a good job I didn't wait any longer. I peed and peed, the mug filling up as I tilted it gradually more upright like an expert barman handling a pint of Guinness. And it wasn't stopping. For one awful moment it looked like the mug would overflow and I'd soak the bed. I couldn't believe I was going to piss myself. I'd come so far with the indignity of bedpans and pee bottles,

I couldn't blow all that by filling a mug until it overflowed onto my bed. But then the pee started to slow, easing from a stream to a dribble. The mug was almost up to the brim by now but the dribble finally stopped and I sat there holding a mugful of urine. Carefully, gingerly, I put it down on the cabinet, feeling every kind of relief.

That was about the extent of my achievement. Not able to move off the bed I looked down at my legs; one in a frame, the other wrapped by a swollen-looking bandage, and still couldn't believe I was there. In a few days' time the bandage and fixed cast would be off my right ankle and I was looking forward to that. But as I lay there waiting for my wife to come home I had no idea that the visit to the surgery would be the most ignominious point in my recovery.

If I wasn't going to disappear into a wasteland of worry, I knew I had to keep busy. But keeping busy for me means being on a bike somewhere or doing something active, and now the only thing I could really keep active was my mind. Once the cast was off my leg I ought to be able to walk with crutches and I'd be able to drive the Range Rover. I was missing that, and I had my eye on my wife's moped where it seemed to squat temptingly on the drive. It didn't have footpegs; it had a central well like a scooter, and I reckoned it wouldn't be long before I'd be able to get on it and ride.

But I wasn't even upright yet. To keep my mind occupied I picked up a book on superbike racing written by

Keith Code, an ex-racer turned mentor who runs the California Superbike School.

A few years back I interviewed him for the BBC programme *Holiday*. I asked him how he got into bikes and he told me he used to buy the publication *Motorcycle News* back in the day, getting it mailed over to the States so he could get all the gen on the racing scene in Europe. A contemporary of Barry Sheene and Steve Parrish, he told me that before he became a racer his job was to make platform shoes for female porn stars.

For a moment, I thought he was joking. 'Keith,' I said, 'you're kidding me, right? What did you really do?'

'I made shoes for porn stars. Really.'

'Are you serious?' I still wasn't sure if he was winding me up, but he looked me in the eye and made an open-handed gesture.

'It's true,' he said. 'I used to make the shoes then go and visit the set to see my creations in action. If you think about it, the only items of clothing a porn star will leave on when she's working are her shoes, and they're normally platforms or stilettoes.'

After a while discussing the ins and outs of the porn industry we got on to racing, and Keith admitted that he was never good enough to take on the likes of Barry Sheene and Kenny Roberts. Those were the days when racers were real playboys though, so his former occupation would have fitted perfectly. Barry was the poster boy of bikes and James Hunt his counterpart in Formula One. The two of them were really good friends and in many ways they were alike.

I remember being in a West End restaurant with Olly one night not long after we started dating. We sat down opposite each other at the end of this long table, and as I glanced at another table close by I recognised one of its occupants as Damon Hill. Damon's a good friend these days, but at the time I didn't know him or the people he was with, not to speak to anyway. I recognised them alright: Murray Walker, Michael Schumacher and David Coulthard, plus the legend that was Barry Sheene. Later when I finished my meal I got up to go to the loo, and when I came back Barry was in my seat chatting up Olly. That was nothing new; chatting up beautiful women was part of Barry's life. As I walked up behind him I heard him tell her how he lived in Australia these days, and asked if she would like to come out. Very coolly I tapped him on the shoulder and he looked up.

'Barry,' I said. 'My girlfriend won't come to Australia with you – but I will.'

He took a moment to look me up and down. 'Naw,' he said, and got up from my seat.

It's not like that anymore. With everything so sanitised and corporate, and every racer taught how to be media savvy, everyone seems more programmed, almost – more aloof. That was Keith Code's era though, the mid to late 70s, and you can see it in him even now. He's a very cool, very assured-looking guy. I took his racing class and learned a hell of a lot that I thought I already knew. Like a lot of ex-racers or sportsmen who weren't quite at the top of their game, Keith knew how it should be done and as far as coaching is concerned he's one of the all-time greats. Together with the rest of the class, I followed him on the track and for the first few laps we weren't allowed to use the brakes. He wanted to show us that racing is all about the right speed at the right time, and very quickly I learned that as soon as you tip your bike into a corner you're already slowing, regardless of whether you're using your brakes or not. It's all about balance, control and target fixation. He's the kind of guy who's made a science out of racing and broken it down to where every area of your time on the track can be analysed as an individual exercise.

As such, Keith's one of those people who's really added something to the art of racing. There have been a few down the years and one of them was Barry. When he started out, riders were pretty upright in the saddle – there was no hanging off the bike with your knee on the ground whilst cornering – and the generation before him, Mike Hailwood et al, didn't move on the bike at all. It took a rider like Barry to realise the more upright the bike was the better it could get out of a corner, because more of the tyre was on the road. The only way to achieve that was to shift your weight from side to side and use your knee as a balance point, but that meant it was close to (or scraping) the tarmac. In those early days the racers used to strap all sorts of everything to their leathers in order to stop them grinding their kneecaps.

Keith Code took the art of cornering to another level altogether. Much of what he writes in his books is about what goes on in your head. When he discusses how to make the perfect corner he doesn't start with the entry but the exit. He maintains that if you work on getting your exit perfect then the rest of the corner will take care of itself. The exit is the target area and from there you can work backwards to the entry stage by stage. Target fixation is key. For example, if there's a big crack in the tarmac on a particular corner you will always focus on that, meaning you'll steer towards it. By the time you look up again you're already three bike-lengths further on and all you're doing is playing catch-up. The corner is ruined and you've lost time you didn't need to lose. If you're on the road and you get a corner wrong the consequences could be much more serious.

By focusing on the exit rather than the entry you ensure that your target area, the point on which you're focusing, is the final part of the corner – and not that crack. You're looking ahead, but what's directly in front of you is no longer the focal point. It's exactly the same principle when you're riding off-road.

Keith talks a lot about MotoGP racer Valentino Rossi, who some refer to as the 'GOAT' (Greatest of All Time). He may well be, though I've always thought it's hard to compare different machinery and different eras. There was a time when people who talked about Rossi might say they'd met him or spoken to him, but he's become such a legend, has such an aura nowadays that you're more likely to hear people say that they were in the presence of Valentino Rossi rather than that they met him. The MotoGP commentators refer to him and a few others like Marquez and Lorenzo as aliens rather than mere mortals – because they're so far ahead of the rest of us, the way they approach their craft is so different, that it's as if they're from another planet. A racer like Valentino has half a dozen different racing lines instead of the usual one that most of us have. Watch closely when you see him on a MotoGP bike; you can see how he's working the track through the cameras they have mounted on the bikes, particularly the one that focuses on his eyes. Valentino isn't looking at the corner he's riding, but at least one corner ahead, sometimes two, and picking what line he carries accordingly. Rarely does he get any part of it wrong. It's what separates the great from the good; and Rossi isn't a nine-time World Champion for nothing.

Lying on the bed back home it was good to refresh my mind about the art of racing. It was the motivation I needed to start getting well. You're never too old (or too injured) to learn. Track days are where you can hone your skills for the road; what you learn when taking a corner is put into practice in your everyday riding. There are always instructors on track days and the best thing any rider can do, no matter how good they think they are, is listen to what those instructors tell you. Once I was on a track day being instructed by Neil Hodgson, former British and World Superbike Champion. He taught me a huge amount, as did both Leon Haslam and his father Ron. I learned masses from people like Matt Llewellyn and the late David Jefferies, who used to ride for the Superstock team Ewan and I ran with Claire Ritchie in 1998. I'd met Ewan only a year before and we got involved in trying to raise money for the team so we could go full-time racing. I remember the Brands Hatch round of the 1998 World Superbike Championship; we were with Claire when Suzy Perry came down to interview us. Ewan made the point that though we were trying to use our status within the film business to help bring sponsorship in, we were also bike-mad racing fans ourselves. He was only 27 then and I was coming up on 32 and we spent the next couple of years involved in the British Superstock series. The team was called 'Generace' and we ran various different bikes, including the then brand new Yamaha R1.

You'd be amazed at the number of riders I talk to who tell me they don't need any input from anyone. But the majority of the instructors have more experience in one finger than most road riders will achieve in a lifetime so we do ourselves a disservice if we ignore them. I remember one outing at Donington Park when former British and World Champion Ron Haslam told me my lap times were close to some of his instructors. He seemed pretty impressed and even asked if I'd consider instructing. I was gobsmacked, my head suddenly so large I could barely get my helmet on. He offered to take me out two-up so he could show me the lines he used, and I accepted immediately. When we got back my head had returned to its normal size and I was more than a little sheepish. I might've been quick(ish) but with even with me as a pillion Ron was a full ten seconds faster than my fastest lap.

Keith Code is right: so much of riding is in the mind. I remember being at the Dakar and people were banging on about being 'bike-fit'. At first I didn't really understand what they meant; I thought you just had to be fit physically. But what they were talking about is more like experience – the more time you spend riding, the more information you absorb and the less effort you have to expend. It's about rhythm and mindset, and how any time on a bike increases your 'fitness' to ride. It doesn't matter if it's off-road or on a racetrack, it's all better understanding of how the machines react. Off-road you spend much of your time standing on the pegs, and it's all about keeping your body upright and allowing the bike to move around. On the track, you're hanging off the bike as much as possible but the bike needs to remain as upright and stable as you can keep it.

Ironically, despite all the off-road riding I'd done in Ireland as a kid, I failed my test the first time I took it. I couldn't believe it. I'd had the Yamaha DT100, the YZ250 (however briefly) and after that a 125. When it came to take my test I rented a bike, and on the way to the centre I realised the rear light wasn't working. Really irritated, I stopped at a petrol station to change the bulb which took precious time. I was getting more and more exasperated, and when I finally got to the centre I was not only late but in a mental melt-down. Of course I failed; I couldn't make the U turn without putting my foot down, I was going too fast – everything went to rat-shit.

The second time I was determined that wouldn't happen so I gave myself three hours to get there. The tester followed in a car rather than on another motorbike, keeping in contact by radio; it felt weird because when it came to junctions I couldn't filter to the front of the traffic. It didn't matter, though, because I remember the relief as well as joy I felt when he told me I'd actually passed. He was a good guy and could see I was more than comfortable on a bike, and in many ways he helped me out. When it came to the emergency stop, for example, he told me to ride around the block at a certain speed and he would step out between parked cars with his hand up. I'd then do the emergency stop which is brake, brake, brake then at the last minute pull in the clutch to stop the bike from stalling. He suggested I go quite slowly because if I skidded at all I'd fail.

'Twenty miles an hour,' he said, 'keep it around 20 miles an hour.'

He told me that in the old days the testers used to hide between the cars and at the last minute jump out and hold their hand up. That really was an emergency stop, but one day the tester heard the bike approach and jumped out – only to find it wasn't his student, it was a courier, who ploughed straight into him.

It occurred to me as I re-read Keith's book that after I started out riding that retro Zephyr I then got heavily into sportsbikes. It's the same for most of us I suppose, an age thing maybe. I had various GSX-Rs, the first of which I trashed while taking the slip road from the M4 at Slough. You know the one I mean? It's a left-hand bend that goes on and on, then comes back on itself and you can get your knee down. I peeled into it at speed and cranked the bike over until I was scraping my knee in a perfect arc. It was fantastic, a real racing move. I was spot on – until the back end stepped out and the bike went spiralling down the road to crash into a bollard.

I had a few more Suzukis after that as well as a Yamaha R1, then it was Ewan's Ducati 748SP. Yellow and white, the little brother to the iconic 916, the bike had been given to him as a 'wrap present' when he finished filming his first *Star Wars* movie with George Lucas. It was a typical Ewan thing to do; I was down on my luck and he's always been a generous-hearted person.

I've known him nearly 20 years now, though recently we haven't seen as much of each other as we'd like. That's the nature of the movie business; you're always off somewhere shooting and it was a film set where we first met. The night before the first significant day of filming, we were in a pub that bore more than a passing resemblance to someone's living room. Ewan was playing a Dutch gardener in *The Serpent's Kiss*, and I was playing the secretary. I'd seen him in *Shallow Grave* and *Trainspotting*, but this was the first time we had actually spoken. It was the kick-off party and we were supposed to temper it a little but I don't think anybody did. I saw Ewan at the bar and knew he rode motorbikes so I went over and introduced myself.

'I'm Charley,' I said. 'I hear you ride bikes?'

'Yeah.' He spoke with a little hesitation in his voice as if he wasn't sure about this long-haired stranger right in his face.

'Guzzi, isn't it?'

He nodded. 'That's right, a '78, 850.'

As shooting went on and the movie blossomed, so did our friendship; born out of a mutual love of motorbikes. We started talking about riding together through Spain or somewhere one day when our children were older. That was in the early days and nothing really came of it until Ewan bought a map of the world from a bookshop in Primrose Hill. It was on a whim, and when he got home he spread it out on the pool table in the basement of his house. Right away his imagination started to wander and it wasn't long before riding together in Spain was forgotten in favour of a trip to China, because that's where his wife Eve grew up. Of course China borders Mongolia, and that also appealed to Ewan with the history of Genghis Khan and the largest empire the world has ever known, stretching halfway across Europe. As Ewan traced that line on the map he considered the border between Mongolia and Siberia. From there it was the Asia–Pacific Rim and only a short hop to Alaska. I think that was the moment the idea of a world trip was born and it happened to be the moment I phoned him.

'What're you doing?' I said.

'I'm looking at a map of the world I bought from a shop in Primrose Hill,' he said. 'Charley, I think you and Olly better come over for dinner.'

We went that same evening and got into a serious discussion straight away. Ewan told me his idea was to ride all the way around the world, and I was really excited. I remember thinking that when you look at a map the distances you're actually talking about are only a few centimetres on a bit of paper. That's how it looked there on his pool table; Europe to Russia, Mongolia and a short hop across the Bering Strait from Siberia, and we would finish the trip in New York. Ewan thought there was a book in it, maybe a TV series as well, so I had the chance of making some money. This was 2003, and if we were really going to do it he had a couple of films to make before we could set off. After that he said he would take at least three months away from work and we could leave the following spring.

Both Olly and Eve were up for the idea so our first port of call was a bookshop and a copy of *The Adventure Motorcycling Handbook*. We looked at it together and the very first word of the very first chapter was 'Prepare'. It went on to inform us that if we really were planning to make such a trip then we needed to allow at least a year for preparation. I remember the look on Ewan's face; his LA agent was nervous enough that he was taking three months out of his acting career, let alone a whole year.

'It'll be alright,' I said. 'We can do this, Ewan, we don't need a year to prepare. You go off and do what you have to, I'll find a TV producer and we'll be all set up when you get back.'

Brave words, Charley; and from the mouth of a chronic dyslexic. Of course, I forgot all about it and that nearly came back to haunt me.

It was April of 2003 and I was at home in Fulham when the phone rang. 'It's me,' Ewan said. 'Forget three months, Charley, I've booked myself out for eight. January to August next year, they don't like it but I'm committed. So, you said you'd find a producer – what've you done about the TV show?'

Fuck, I thought. *My chance to get back in the game and I've only gone and forgotten.*

'Everything is cool,' I said. 'Nothing's firmed up yet but I've been talking to lots of people.'

'Great, when can I meet them?'

'Leave it with me, Ewan. I'll set something up and get back to you.'

When I hung up the phone I just stood there for a moment staring out the window. *What am I going to do now?* I thought. *Eight months he said, and he's already told his agents.*

Fortunately, I'd been at a party just a week or so before and met Russ Malkin, who introduced himself as a TV producer. People have described Russ as brash and cocky, but he's incredibly measured and calm. He comes across as sure of himself, but that's a prerequisite in this business. Anyway, I had his card so I called him.

'Russ, this is Charley Boorman. We spoke at the party, remember? I mentioned a motorbike trip with Ewan.'

My leg was hurting and I was sitting in an awkward position so I put Keith's book down and adjusted the way I was sitting. I closed my eyes for a moment. I'd noticed how tired I was getting, and that was partially due to the ache and partially the effort it took to move around. Though I was falling asleep at night, I was waking up in the early hours. I tried to rest now, but for some reason I couldn't stop thinking about the rust on the forks of my bobber; it was bugging me, probably because there wasn't anything I could do about it.

Normally when I've got a bit of downtime I go to the lock-up and work on some project or other, but I couldn't even manage that right now. I hate seeing a bike I love showing signs of wear. I told myself I'd deal with it when I was well enough; another project, another waypoint to aim for along with all the others.

I think it was riding that bike – and thinking how cool it looked – that got me involved with the Bike Shed in London. It's a retro café bar complete with bespoke motorcycles for sale as well as retro clothing, helmets and accessories. Spread over four railway arches in Shoreditch, it's a great place to chill out, have a party or business meeting. I'd long since been inspired by the kind of thing Deus Ex Machina were doing in Australia with hand-built retro bike creations, and I tried to get something going with them in Brighton. It didn't happen, but I was undeterred; I looked for opportunities elsewhere and came across one with the Bike Shed.

It's an amazing concept, and if you're ever in the Shoreditch area of London you really have to check it out. What's now a permanent business started as a blog by Anthony 'Dutch' van Someren. He's a really good guy who worked as a creative director in the media and was into KTMs in a big way, though his background was actually dirt bikes. His mates were all bikers; cameramen, producers and TV directors, as much into the uniqueness and aesthetics of the motorbike world as the bikes themselves. Dutch talks about how he grew bored with the latest offerings from the mainstream manufacturers, since for him and his friends it was no longer about horsepower so much as art and culture. Inspired by like-minded souls from different parts of the world they created a group blog – a virtual bike shed – where they posted photos of bespoke motorcycle creations by unknown craftsmen that would otherwise never get an audience. 'Underground blogging', Dutch calls it; the human story behind the art that is a single hand-built, individually designed motorbike. Back then the only place to see any bikes exhibited was the National Exhibition Centre and that was in Birmingham, miles from the London scene. So, from the blog the idea of a separate event was born, a 'pop-up' exhibition where individual bike-builders were accorded the same floor space as Ducati or Triumph, set against a backdrop of art, photography and hospitality. It was held in May 2013 and attended by 3,000 visitors. It proved to be such a success that a second was held that October, and this time 5,000 people came to the Shoreditch studios. From all walks of life, they included a whole host of celebrities (including Brad Pitt) who were beginning to get into this artisanal, cultural crossover scene.

The kind of bikes on display were café racers, brat style and modern scramblers. I was at that event, along with Nicholas Cowell (Simon's brother), who I knew from parents' evenings at the school Doone and Kinvara attended, and it was there we first met Dutch. I'd never met anyone quite like him before, something of a visionary in terms of biking and motorbikes. For a long time he'd had this idea of a fixed location for a shop/café where the culture as well as the mechanics of the biking world could come together as never before. Talking to him I realised that this was just the kind of thing that Nick and I were wanting to be a part of. He and I had been discussing just this kind of crossover. Bike and surf, or street, or art – something that complemented the motorcycling lifestyle. As soon as we started to talking to Dutch we could see he had exactly that kind of vision, and he introduced us to Frederick Lukoff, the CEO of the Stella McCartney brand. The idea of a permanent fixed location was Dutch's baby, but he couldn't pull it together on his own. Frederick was as keen to get involved as we were, so together with a whole bunch of other investors, we backed Dutch's vison as best we could. To cut a long story short, what had been a series of pop-up events became a permanent fixture in Shoreditch. Bikes on display, super-cool clothing; there's even an old fashioned American-style barbershop as featured in the original Bike Shed shows. Even if you're not there to buy you can relax in a different kind of biker café, with Chesterfield sofas and bare brick walls, just soaking in the ambience and culture. And as far as I know it's the only online bike shop that advertises bikes by style rather than manufacturer.

TELSCHE

After a couple of weeks at home I felt so incapacitated it was almost silly. I've never been in such a bad way; infection kept growing up around the pins in my leg and I swabbed them meticulously. I wasn't due to see either of my surgeons again just yet, so I swallowed antibiotics and ordered the Exogen machine I'd been told about in the hospital. It was costly but if it worked then my insurance would cover it. I didn't care about the cost – this was my leg, and every time I felt the tweak of any new tenderness a cold sweat would work its way through me.

I tried to focus on what Ian Hutchinson had achieved; how he'd come back from a worse break than this and not only raced again but learned to use a right-hand gear shift. It might sound simple, but it goes against everything you've ever learned on a bike and to hone that to race speed is incredible. You have to practice and practice, unpick what your brain is telling you then reprogram it again.

I wasn't trying to get to professional racing level, but I was trying to get back on a bike as soon as possible. Having said that, ever since Ron Haslam mentioned my lap times, I've wondered if I haven't missed my vocation. I know he'd been ten seconds quicker than I was, but he's Ron Haslam – he'd spent an entire career racing at the top level. If I'd started when I was young instead of trying to be an actor, who knows what might have happened.

After I finished *The Emerald Forest* my performance in auditions was so inept that I hardly got any jobs in film or TV. I just could not learn the lines, and the thought of doing theatre terrified me. What if I forgot my lines in the middle of a scene with an entire audience watching? What if I started to stammer and stutter? I couldn't deal with that possibility and my frustration was so acute I used to throw the script across the room. My confidence was shot, just as it had been when I first tried to learn to read. My professional world was falling apart and the only roles I could get were in Dad's films or those made by sympathetic friends of the family.

I started to disappear inside myself as I had done when I was a kid. The silences I talk about weren't just to be found in some quiet place; they became part of being on a motorbike. When something was troubling me I'd take off on my bike with the world shut out by the confines of a full-face helmet. I'd ride and ride until I'd come up with some plan to deal with what was bothering me. In the early days it was on that Zephyr, and I remember one time just before the jobs dried up when I was working on a TV movie in west London. We'd just finished a night shoot and instead of going home I took off on my bike and cut through the streets of southwest London. I rode all the way to the M25 then opened it up, and finally stopped at Gatwick Airport. I don't know why I ended up there, but I just turned around and took the same route home. Alone with my thoughts I got back to the house I was sharing with Olly just as she was getting up. That seems so long ago now – we've been together for almost 30 years. I was in my early 20s when we started going out, and 25 when we got married.

In those days, I spent a lot of time with Telsche. She was that much older than me, and Dad always said she was like a second mother to me – maybe even more so after my parents were divorced. Back then, when she lived in Paris, the city was a nightmare for street theft. You couldn't leave anything in a car without the windows being smashed and I had to chain up my bike so much that I could barely undo it.

Telsche always seemed to be more cerebral than the rest of us; I think she got that from Dad. A real bookworm, she loved to read and she worked on film scripts and stuff for the theatre. She loved life and was always full of it, outgoing and a little mischievous with the most fabulous laugh imaginable. I remember when Dad was making *Deliverance,* we were in some café and Telsche and Katrine were outside with these little fairy figures (like Tinkerbell from *Peter Pan*) mounted on sticks. They held them up and made them dance across the window, and Daisy (who was inside with me) was absolutely convinced they were real. That was typical of Telsche even at such a young age – a mix of imagination and humour. There was something about her that met life head on; maybe that was just another trait she inherited, or perhaps it was something she adopted through being 'born twice' after the day she drowned in the pond. Dad thought so; after what happened that day in the garden he always felt she was on borrowed time, and maybe so did she.

When I was growing up I idolised Telsche because she was so good at everything. She was an excellent student and had an aptitude for sports, her forte track and field. She ran very fast, she threw the javelin a long way and she was an excellent horsewoman. I told you about Snowy, the horse who wouldn't take the bridle. Telsche was as fearless as I was; she would ride around the fields standing on his back. We'd bought him from a bunch of travellers, and he really was something. Gentle as a lamb, you could go up to him and crawl between his legs, lie on the ground underneath his belly, walk right up behind him and he'd never even think about kicking you. He couldn't have cared less just as long as you didn't show up with a bridle. I had a motorbike like that, one with a mind of its own; it was as cunning as that horse ever was and the only way you could get it started was if it didn't know you were there. You just had to sneak up, throw yourself on and kick-start it before it realised you were coming.

I spoke earlier about Telsche living with Arnaud Selignac while I was in Paris, appearing in *Nemo*. They didn't stay together; they broke up after he had an affair with one of the stars and it was only a few months later that she met a journalist called Lionel Rotcage. They had been together less than a year when they decided to get married and, again,

I wonder if that wasn't something within Telsche's subconscious. I remember meeting Lionel for the first time when they flew out to Brazil while we were making *The Emerald Forest*. His mother was Régine Rotcage, a famous French nightclub singer born in Belgium who'd sung in France during the years of Nazi occupation.

There was something about Lionel that didn't quite fit with the sister I'd grown up with. The fact that they were going to get married so quickly seemed a little hurried and a little alarming. I remember Dad trying to persuade Telsche to wait at least until the filming was over and we were back from South America. But her mind was made up and they went ahead.

Telsche adored France and all things French; Katrine was the same. I mentioned they were at the Sorbonne on a Cordon Bleu course, though neither of them went into the restaurant business. Katrine acted and Telsche started writing. She was very good, with same kind of gift that Dad has, a similar way with words. He's written or co-written most of the movies he's made down the years, and Telsche worked on a lot of scripts and over time became a kind of script doctor. She was able to translate from French to English and English to French in the same way Katrine can. She had a feel for dialogue, particularly comic dialogue, in both languages. She co-wrote the screenplay for a French film called *Gazon Maudit* which won a French film industry César, the equivalent of a Hollywood Oscar, for its writing.

Telsche was so easy to hang out with, so sensitive towards other people's feelings. When I married Olly I had so little money I had to borrow some from Telsche in order to pay my way, but she'd never let me pay her back. She was always the first person to help out in a crisis, and that's why we were concerned about her marrying someone like Lionel. He just wasn't on that kind of wavelength.

She left Lionel in the early 90s after less than ten years of marriage, and for a while she was almost like a teenager again. She was the old Telsche we'd not seen anything of since she got married. She met a new guy, a French actor called Jean-Michel who was so good-looking it was ridiculous. They saw each other for a while and then the relationship faded into one of just friendship. In her last few years though, Jean-Michel was always there for her.

I think a lot about what Dad used to say; that she was on borrowed time. It's haunting because it turned out to be so prophetic. Still living in Paris, she went to the doctor after a bout of back pain refused to go away and was eventually diagnosed with ovarian cancer. We were devastated. Telsche was the first child, she was larger than life, the girl who could ride a horse standing on its back. She tried absolutely everything, both conventional and alternative treatments, but nothing seemed to be working.

I remember one night when I couldn't sleep in the hospital at Charing Cross. I lay there thinking how Telsche had endured a hysterectomy and stem cell treatment where she spent long periods in an isolation ward with no contact with any of us at all. None of those procedures made any difference so she tried every kind of herbal treatment there was, but none of that had any affect either.

Over the next couple of years she had so many treatments we all thought one of them was bound to work. We hoped against hope that the next course she took would be the one that would finally click, but it wasn't. Towards the end it was harrowing to see my sister, who'd been so full of life, just gradually waste away.

In those last days, she used to read and read as if she could not take in enough information. She loved Agatha Christie in particular but she had a penchant for all the old Penguin books, the ones with the orange and white covers. Lots of different authors, all the classics; she had a stack of them permanently beside her bed.

She was in hospital in London for a while, and I remember coming home from work when I was painting and decorating, and going to visit her on Ewan's old Ducati 748SP. We'd talk about everything and anything except what was to come. Towards the end she left London and went back to Paris. Her flat was in the 14th arrondissement, a beautiful gated community made up of six or seven gorgeous houses. Katrine had been over there for a while with Mum and Dad, then I took a turn staying with her. The French health service was very good; they sent what they called a 'pain doctor' to the apartment with two large cases of drugs and he'd mix a cocktail to make her comfortable. A big-time biker, I remember him turning up with helmet and black leathers and riding an old BMW.

There were three or four days just before she died when Telsche was free of pain. Both Dad and Mum were around but I had a night and a day when it was just the two of us, and I'm so grateful for that. We didn't talk much; we were just able to enjoy each other's company. I think Telsche had the same sense of silence that I did and there's no doubt in those last days that I reverted to my failsafe. I was in her company though, and that's all that mattered. Katrine came back and I returned to London. Things were pretty bad by then and I remember getting a telephone call very early in the morning. I knew what had happened as soon as it rang but it didn't matter. When Dad told me, the shock was so great I felt as if all the air had been sucked from my body. He didn't sound like Dad. His voice was hollow, hopeless and empty. I'd never heard him like that. He'd brought her back to life and now she was gone. He was utterly, completely broken.

I couldn't take it in. My sister was gone and I felt as if all hope had disappeared with her. The world was a dark and bitter place; a light had gone out and would never be lit again. I was a sudden mess, a wreck of a thing, so stunned and numb I couldn't even think, let alone get any words out. I remember finally being able to tell Olly. She and Telsche had been very close and she was as devastated as I was. I didn't go back to bed; I went straight to Kings Cross and got on the Eurostar to Paris. I remember every moment of that journey as if it was yesterday. Staring out the window I seemed to absorb every building, every tree, every piece of road and it all seemed stark and empty.

I got to Telsche's apartment and found so many of her friends already there. Her funeral was attended by literally hundreds of people, most of whom I'd never met. We had an Irish wake with my sweet sister laid out in bed while the party went on around her. It lasted for two full days, an alcohol-fuelled period of reflection, remembrance and celebration. Different groups of people would go into the bedroom and take turns sitting with her. They'd cry, they'd wail…I can hear that sound even now, my sister lying in state with different groups of friends keening like ancient Celts all around her.

The funeral was as well attended as her wake. So many friends, so many people who wished her well – in such a short time on this earth she had touched so many lives. I love her. I miss her, and I visit her grave at Montmartre every chance I get.

After she died we wanted a keepsake, something really personal that would always remind us of Telsche. Initially we weren't sure what to do; then someone suggested we have a cast made of her hands as she lay in repose. It seemed like an excellent idea so we spoke to Philippe Berry, a great friend of the family and an amazing artist. He crafted a perfect bronze cast of my sister's hands for each of us so we'd always have something of Telsche.

As time's gone by the pain has eased of course, but you never really heal from something like that. Dad in particular never got over it and I suppose he never will. Children aren't meant to die before their parents. I'll never forget my sister.

When I rode around the world with Ewan, she was with me in spirit – it was the same when we rode through Africa. It was as if she was on the back of the bike, leaning over my shoulder and encouraging me like she always used to. It took me seven years to take her telephone number off my phone. Every time I went to do it I couldn't because it felt as if I was abandoning her and confirming she was no longer part of my life.

She left a young daughter behind; my niece Daphne, who was living with her father Lionel by then because Telsche was too sick to be able to look after her by herself. When the funeral was over and Telsche's affairs all taken care of, Mum went back to Paris to make sure Daphne had someone from our side of the family to be there for her, if only in the background. She wanted to give her as much reassurance as possible as Daphne had lost her mother, and she ended up staying for the next ten years. That wasn't easy because Mum was German and, though a very capable woman, she didn't speak any French. Having grown up in rural Germany she had come to London and managed to learn English, but learning another language at a much later stage of life was beyond her. Whenever she and Daphne were out together it was Daphne who would translate. They used to go to the same café all the time and the waiters got to know them really well. They adored Daphne. She was only seven or eight back then, angelic, with blonde curly hair, she looked like Shirley Temple and the way she could flit from French to English just blew the waiters away.

Mum was determined that Daphne would grow up with as much emotional security as possible, and the fact that she herself might be lonely wasn't going to get in the way. It's funny; as I write this book I realise that my dad is such a massive character he dominates in a way that my mum doesn't. But she was a huge figure in all her children's lives. She and Dad divorced not long before Olly and I got married, and Dad went on to have another family – my three half-siblings Lola, Lily Mae and Lee, the latter named after Dad's great friend Lee Marvin. We don't see as much of them as we would like, but then I suppose we're all very busy with our own lives. There was a Christmas a few years back when we went over and I managed to get not just my two kids on a motorbike with me, but my three half-siblings as well. Dad's got a photo somewhere of the six of us tottering around the grounds of the house in County Wicklow. That's where Lola, Lily Mae and Lee grew up, the same house that I did, until Dad's second marriage broke up.

Dad carried on the tradition of using his children in movies rather than find a child actor he didn't know. I remember Lola was in *The Tailor of Panama*, a movie based on John le Carré's novel that featured Daniel Radcliffe before he was made famous through the *Harry Potter* series.

Mum was always a large part of the success my dad made of his life in the movies and he's always been aware of that. In those years after Telsche died, however, I think she was isolated, a little apart from the rest of the world because she was unable to grasp the language. She didn't care; she'd made a commitment and was a constant and reassuring presence for Daphne throughout the rest of her childhood. Daphne lives in London now – she's stable, married and very happy. My mum never got married again and died a few years ago after a lengthy illness. We all miss her very much. For so many years she was the life and soul of the party, always in the kitchen, always so welcoming. I miss her when I'm preparing for dinner parties or when friends just show up out of the blue – we're very much open house, and I know I get that spirit of hospitality from her.

POLISHING THE
STEPS

Telsche always encouraged me to tackle life head on and despite the severity of this setback, I was determined to do just that. The next hurdle was the partial cast on my right ankle. We were due to see the surgeon and I was full of anticipation as Olly got the Micra ready and loaded Ziggy. I was in the wheelchair at the front door and she pushed me across the drive to where I could hoist myself from the chair to the passenger seat. I still couldn't put any weight on my left foot but that was largely due to the condition of the right. Hopefully by the end of today all that would have changed.

We drove across town to Fitzhardinge Street where the ankle surgeon has his practice. We were due to see Andy Roche who operated on me at the Chelsea and Westminster, and the clinic is in one of those old-style London houses that were converted into offices. We parked close by, Olly brought the chair around again and I manhandled myself out of the car. She wheeled me along the pavement to the black railings and white stone fascia, only to find the door was at the top of four London-style concrete steps.

'There's got to be a ramp,' I said. 'He's an orthopaedic surgeon – patients must show up in wheelchairs all the time.'

There was no sign of one though, so Olly rang the bell and went in. Meanwhile I was just sitting there as various pedestrians passed by. Watching them go I thought how simple a thing like walking really was and how much we take it for granted. It's funny, we often wonder what we'd do if we lost our job or had no money, but it's the simplest things that affect us the most.

A few minutes later Olly was back. 'There is no ramp, Charley,' she told me. 'They said the council won't let them have a permanent one but there's no temporary one either.'

I looked at her. She looked at me and we both wondered what we were going to do. 'Is there anyone inside who can help me?'

'Just the receptionist, but she's got to man the phone.'

I stared at the steps wondering how on earth I was going to get up them. 'Maybe we can get the chair up?' I suggested. 'There're only four steps and they're not too steep – if you turn the chair around, maybe you can pull it up backwards.'

Olly had a go but to no avail. Even shallow as they looked, the steps were far too steep. She tried to tilt the chair and bump me up the first one but the combination of me and chair was too heavy and the angle still too acute. I sat in silence, not quite believing they didn't have a temporary ramp. But they didn't and I was left with no choice but to get out of the chair and try to haul myself up.

I asked Olly to push the chair up to the bottom step and then I levered myself out. People were still passing by on both sides of the street and one or two looked on as I shuffled around on my arse. Now I had my back to the first step and I took my weight on my hands and tried to ease myself up. The only part of my feet I could use was my left heel. I could press that against the ground to create some leverage but it took just about all my strength. I managed to get to the first step and rested a moment before trying again. It was agonising, but I took the weight a second time, lifted my left leg up by the frame and so managed to get to the second step. There I sat with my legs hanging like some dead weight. I was sweating, and it was in my eyes. I've never felt as helpless or pathetic in my life as when I was polishing that step with my bum then using all my strength trying to work my way up to the next one. There were quite a few onlookers now but I ignored them, took the weight on my hands again and made the third step. I had to rest for a moment; my legs were really aching now and not just my left, but also the right.

Finally I got to the top step and Olly came up with the chair. But I wasn't done yet. There was a final step where the front door fitted and I couldn't get back in the chair until I'd negotiated that. So, I had to shuffle across the width of the top step on my bum. I had to creep backwards to the door while Olly went inside with the chair. Then I had to take the weight on the flat of my hands all over again and ease myself over that last lip. From there I shuffled backwards until the hall opened out and Olly could turn the chair. I still couldn't get in though – I had nothing to lever myself up with. All the time the receptionist was standing there looking helpless and really embarrassed.

I felt degraded, hunched like some half-human on the floor. Olly spotted a padded stool with four short legs in the reception area by the magazines. She brought it over and I asked her to turn it on its side. Resting my arm on the edge of the stool, I was able to lever myself up until finally I was back in the chair. By now I was red in the face and feeling so utterly wretched I could've cried. The ignominy of having to shuffle all the way from the pavement on my arse was the lowest point I'd reached by far. It took a moment to gather my emotions and I sat just staring at the wall.

Olly was flicking through a magazine, just as frustrated and angry as I was. I stared out the window to the street and saw a courier pull up and I was almost in tears.

A buzzer sounding on the receptionist's desk shook me from my despondency and the woman told us the surgeon was ready for us. Now we had another struggle as Olly wheeled me along the narrow corridor to a lift at the back of the building. It wasn't very big and with my leg extended we could barely fit in. Finally the door closed and we went up to another corridor and then into the treatment room. The surgeon apologised about the entrance, explaining that he'd been trying to get something done about some kind of ramp ever since he set up in the offices. I told him to forget it. It didn't matter. I really didn't care anymore, I just wanted to see what he thought of my ankle when he took off the bandages.

He unwrapped them carefully, then pried away the solid cast that had been fitted to the back and side of my right leg. I was watching every movement and when I saw my foot I almost cried out. It was terrible, a sort of mishmash of grey skin and crimson blood vessels, and it looked as if it had been dead for a while. But it wasn't dead; the surgeon told me that it was actually doing fine.

'It's looking good,' he said. 'Don't worry about the colour or how flaky the skin appears – that's normal. The lateral wound and the arthroscopies are healing beautifully.'

I half-raised an eyebrow at that. It looked like a dead man's foot, and anything but beautiful to me.

He had me move the ankle as much as I could and asked if I was in any pain. I wasn't, and I could move the joint a little. That was encouraging and he said it was a vast improvement.

'The swelling is minimal,' he stated. 'There's no neurovascular deficit, and the pin wound from Portugal has healed really well. There's still a little fresh blood here and there but no clear liquid at all.'

He dressed the wound again with an absorbent dry dressing then put Mepore on the rest. That's a long-lasting adhesive dressing that doesn't need to be changed that often, and I'd had them before. There was still a small wound at the front of the ankle and he told me that until it was fully healed I had to keep the area dry.

Then he hit me with the 'Beckham boot'. Not literally; he just produced it, and I had no idea that was what he'd had in mind. It was an Aircast, one of those lightweight plastic boots you see footballers hobbling around in all the time. 'Charley,' he said. 'You've got to keep it on til I see you in four weeks' time.'

I stared at him and I stared at the boot that he'd fitted on. Already it felt hot and awkward, really cumbersome despite the relative lack of weight. I stared at the frame on my other leg and thought how difficult sleeping had been already, and how impossible it would be now.

'I have to sleep in this?' I said.

He nodded. 'Don't think about any exercises yet; I want you to keep the ankle as still as you can. You're going to see Mr Nathwani before I see you again, I'll ask him to check the pin wound for me and we'll go from there.'

It was a blow I hadn't forseen. I don't know what I'd expected when he told me he'd be taking the cast off, but back in the car I was as low as I'd ever been, the ignominy of those steps and now a Beckham boot that I'd have to sleep in with the frame already so awkward on my other leg. I was really beginning to question whether I'd ever walk properly again. It was serious, my mood as bad as anything I've felt in the years since Telsche died.

Hospitals were on my mind as we drove home from the ankle surgeon. I had upcoming appointments at the Lindo Wing of St Mary's in Paddington, and despite the hopes for some sort of mobility, I had this boot to deal with as well. It just seemed to be one thing after another and it didn't feel like I was making any progress at all.

I found myself reliving the moments I could remember before the crash and wondered if there was any way I could've avoided it. There was no point thinking about that though, no point going over anything that had happened because I couldn't change any of it now. I had to stay positive and focused. I had to keep in mind that my whole life revolved around motorbikes so all I could do was suck this up and make sure I not only walked again but was fit to ride.

Lying on the bed back at my house with both legs off the ground again, I had to take a moment to remind myself that I had actually ridden a motorbike around the world. That was a hell of an achievement, but I hadn't left it at that; I'd raced the Dakar and ridden from John O'Groats to Cape Town as well. The reminder was incredibly important to me. I'm a great believer that action is the antidote for despair and though I couldn't be physically active now, I could remember when I was and strive to be so again.

It was true I'd achieved a lot, but that first expedition with Ewan proved to be a real watershed moment in my life.

I barely knew Russ Malkin, but after Ewan called to ask if I'd come up with a decent producer I called Russ then set up a meeting where we could discuss the proposal for our expedition. Obviously it was Ewan's name that had caught his attention in the first place and he was keen to see what was planned. As it turned out Ewan was delayed on his way to the meeting, then he couldn't get there at all, and I think Russ was beginning to wonder if I actually knew him.

Fortunately Ewan made the next meeting and Russ finally found out I wasn't full of shit. We talked about the ride we'd discussed and a possible book and the kind of homespun TV show we wanted to create, which in those days hadn't really been done. The most important thing was maintaining control – and that's no easy feat in the TV or movie business, believe me. Ewan particularly had learned the hard way. A few years earlier he'd made a film about polar bears in a town called Churchill, on the Hudson Bay in Canada. He didn't have control and the production company edited the footage in a way he wasn't happy with and sold it to broadcasters all over the world. They made a mint, but it wasn't the money that annoyed Ewan, it was the lack of control.

We needed some semblance of autonomy so Russ brought in David Alexanian, an American director and producer. They were old friends and David had already made a few low-budget films. He'd made money on Wall Street and that gave him the kind of independence all serious filmmakers crave. The most important thing about David though was that he was a biker and would protect the integrity of what we were trying to do. Two mates on motorbikes fulfilling a dream, an adventure, an expedition where nothing is planned and every obstacle overcome through friendship, teamwork and passion.

After that things really began to kick into gear. That September, Russ, David and I flew to Sydney to hook up with Ewan who was finishing the third instalment of the *Star Wars* prequel series. We hired two Yamaha Super Ténérés much like the one Jason had owned, and set off for the outback. Over the next few days we shot a 'sizzle' reel, a taster video we could show to the companies we were talking to in a bid for a TV deal.

As soon as we got back from Australia Russ started talking to various TV companies. He's a single-minded, phlegmatic character with the kind of manner that gets things done. After a few abortive meetings with various stations he was able to get a commitment that would keep the production as Ewan and I had planned.

It was something that hadn't been done on television; two mates, two motorbikes, trekking across the world without any gimmicks or unnecessary additions. I remember one outfit wanted to own all the footage their cameraman filmed. That wasn't something we were going to agree to. We had Ewan's experience in the Hudson Bay as our yardstick so ownership wasn't up for grabs.

We talked to a few different crews and couldn't believe how much red tape there seemed to be surrounding most of them. Jobsworths, almost; people going on about 'health and safety' provisos and downtime, regular breaks. No, there would be no breaks, regular or otherwise. This was a marathon and whoever filmed it had to get that. We'd already decided that the best way to achieve the kind of footage we wanted was for the main cameraman to be on a motorbike. We'd have a backup truck (it would be foolish not to), but the main filming would be done from the bikes. I already knew the camera would be rolling 24/7;

that was the only way to keep it real. After much consultation and sifting through resumes and CVs, we wound up with Claudio von Planta. Again, it was Russ who found him. A bike-riding trailblazer, he had interviewed Osama Bin Laden when he was fighting the Russians with the Mujahideen.

David Alexanian was trying to broker a TV deal for us in LA. He had clout and money, and I remember sitting down with Olly talking about how little cash I had compared to the rest of these guys. Ewan was a movie star, Russ a TV producer – they were all pretty solvent. I was anything but, and right around then we were having a loft conversion done on the house where we lived in Fulham. We'd borrowed the money for that and there would be nothing coming in because I was going to be away for months.

Olly had to deal with it. Our bedroom was pretty much out of commission all the time I was gone and she ended up sleeping on the sofa. She had two young children to take care of by herself and it wasn't as if she wasn't working. The money was the big deal; I think I had about £4,000 in the bank saved from my work as a painter and decorator, but that was all. We still hadn't got all the deals done for the TV and I was worried about how Olly was going to cope. This was a massive gamble; I was walking away from my only source of income and yet she was behind me all the way. I had no idea if the book or TV show would appeal to anyone and the chances were I'd be looking for a job as soon as I got home.

I know how fickle the entertainment industry can be. What one person thinks is going to succeed doesn't work for someone else, and no one really knows what's commercial until it is. I had no real concept of it as a kid. Right up until Dad made *Excalibur* I had no grasp of the world he moved in. By then I was 14 and it was only when the film showed at Cannes that I understood the size of this business, my dad's place in it and just how capricious it could be. I had a small part playing young Mordred, but Dad was keen for me to understand more than just my role so he got me some work with a guy called Terry English. He was responsible for the armour the actors wore in the film, and all of it was handcrafted.

Excalibur was a retelling of the story of King Arthur, a mammoth production with some stalwarts of the British film industry appearing. But it was the sets and costumes, and particularly the armour, that inspired a 14-year-old boy like me. My armour was gold. Not literally; it was aluminium sprayed with gold paint, because aluminium is light enough to wear. It's also soft and can be shaped and moulded, which we did after every battle scene as Terry taught me how to repair and panel beat. When I wasn't filming I'd work with the rest of the armoury department fixing the breastplates and loose armour. There was always lots to do because the fight scenes were protracted and brutal, with young Irish extras bashing the shit out of each other every day. The whole thing was filmed close to where we lived and Dad had roped in young men from the area, all of whom could ride horses. I probably wasn't very good and the work only went on for about a week, but I learned an awful lot from Terry and put some of it into practice when it came to building motorbikes later.

Dad directed of course, and I wasn't the only one of his children in the film. Katrine played Igrayne, and there's a great scene where she's dancing during a feast and all the knights are thumping their fists on the tables. A guy called Robert Addie played Mordred when he was older and, thinking about it now, I probably only got the part because I had a passing resemblance to him.

Most of the scenes I appeared in were filmed in a section of ancient oak forest on our friend Eva Fielder's land. (As well as having been to school with my twin sister Daisy, Eva now runs the Key4Life charity my wife volunteers for.) We used polo ponies for the big scenes because they're trained to ride in close proximity to other horses when that's not a natural situation for them to be in. They could also turn on a sixpence and could be controlled one-handed, which we needed because the knights were wielding swords. But before we could do any of that, we had to get them used to the sound and shine of the armour. We did it in stages, each actor mounting their horse with just the leg sections fitted first, then the arms, and finally breastplate and helmet. I remember the stables the first morning as the cast came clanking past the stalls. The horses were going crazy, whinnying and nickering, some of them rearing up on their hind legs. Every horse in the stables was really freaked out, or at least every one save mine. He didn't seem to be bothered by the armour at all. He didn't give a shit. All he wanted was the hay.

Dad arranged for riding lessons at a school in Bray. I'd been riding Snowy bareback for as long as I could remember, but I had no real saddle technique so I had to go as well. Making that film was amazing fun and a great experience generally. I learned masses about the movie business, but also about my dad in a completely different role. He's a hard taskmaster and working with him is far from an easy ride. Despite the breaks it might look as though I've been getting, he was tougher on his children than anyone else on the set.

Having said that, he's pretty hard on everyone. He expects a hell of a lot of himself and of anyone working for him. If someone isn't up to scratch, or whinges or criticises, he goes for the throat.

When we were in Brazil making *The Emerald Forest* there was this one little guy working as 'key grip'. That's the person who secures the equipment for each take, who looks after the camera, the tripods and the piece of track the camera rolls on. Very early on we trekked up this steep section of jungle to a beautiful waterfall, then made our way across the rushing river from one jagged rock to the next. We had porters and Sherpas carrying all this expensive Panavision camera gear and it took forever to get where dad wanted to go. When we made it to the spot, he waded up to his waist in the water and checked the vista through the hand-held viewfinder.

'Yes,' he muttered. 'That's the shot.' Turning to the Grip he told him to secure the camera in the water exactly where he'd been standing. The Grip looked at him as if he'd gone mad. Hands on hips he started muttering about how this was no way to make a film and that trying to secure such an expensive camera in the river was lunacy.

He just did not understand. That was the shot Dad wanted and that was the shot he would have. A massive argument erupted and the Grip was in Dad's face. That was like a red rag to a bull. Dad told the guy he was fired. If he wasn't prepared to make the shot in the way he'd been instructed, he was off the set. The Grip declared that Dad would never find anyone to take his place at such short notice and Dad assured him he'd have a queue lined up in less than 24 hours. He kicked the guy out there and then. He watched him walk away and told the other members of the crew that if any of them helped him get off the mountain they'd lose their jobs as well.

When it came to the shot itself, Dad was tougher on us than anyone. We only ever had one take whereas most of the other actors got five or six. Sometimes if we were really lucky he might stretch it to two, but generally it was just the one. We had to learn how to do it right first time. Though I didn't know it then, that would stand me in good stead for the kind of TV shows I would go on to do.

We all went to Cannes when *Excalibur* came out and it was only in that moment I fully realised who my father really was. There were paparazzi everywhere, a melee around the steps, and I got swamped in the rush. This was my dad's movie and everybody wanted to talk to him. It was the very first time I really understood: this was his world and he was very good at what he did. I was immensely proud of him.

The crowd was so dense I literally couldn't force my way into the theatre. I was beginning to get pissed off. The others were ahead and I was starting to worry I wouldn't get in because nobody would know who I was. I remember pushing and shoving but not making any progress. Then this arm appeared over the heads of the people blocking my way. Fingers extended, the hand sought me out and grabbed me by the shoulder. It was my dad, and he dragged me through the mass of people into the theatre.

That was the first time I'd seen the film and I was really excited. I had a good part, a speaking part, and when it came to my lines I was all geared up, mouthing them over and over. There I was, young Mordred, son of Morgana and Arthur, dressed in my golden armour and laughing at this hapless knight. 'You seek what Arthur wants? This thing they call the grail?' The lines came from the mouth of the boy in the golden mask, but something was wrong. Something was odd; it didn't sound like me speaking and I couldn't work out why. As I sat there staring at the screen I could feel the intensity of someone's gaze. It was my dad, sitting a couple of seats away. I looked at him and he looked at me. Then I knew what was wrong. It was a girl's voice; my sister Telsche, he'd dubbed her instead of me – even the laughter was Telsche.

Dad told me he'd explain it all to me later, though I'm not sure he ever did. The fact is that because there had been so much noise during the making of the movie, what with the horses, the clash of armour and the wind machine, the entire sound track had to be redone. I'm talking about all the actors' lines, the music, every sound effect from the horses' hooves to people walking on gravel or the swish of a sword through the air. Along with everyone else I'd been into the studio to lip-sync my scene but I hadn't realised it didn't come out very well. Rather than get me back for another go, Dad replaced my voice with my sister's. I get that I suppose – the lines have to be spoken well – but the least he could've used a bloke's voice.

I had a ball making that film and there's one scene that will remain imprinted on my mind forever. The beautiful, adorable Helen Mirren, who played my mother in the movie, rubbing oil all over me while wearing this figure-hugging white outfit. It blew my mind then and still does if I think about it now. Helen's a wonderful woman. Not long ago I was in a restaurant and spotted her just as I was leaving. I went over to say hello and she threw her arms wide to embrace me. 'Ah,' she said. 'My son, my son. It's been so long since I've seen you.'

Anyway, we were talking about the run up to *Long Way Round* and the money (or lack of it) coming into the Boorman household. I remember talking to David about insurances and things like that, the various costs that cropped up as the day of our departure grew ever closer. In the end he spoke to the others and they made sure I had money from the initial advance on the book so everything would be covered.

I remember the day we left as if it was yesterday. Ewan and I on these massive great BMWs, all kitted out for the marathon that lay ahead. We were going to attempt 20,000 miles over 108 days, passing through 19 different time zones before finally, eventually, if the gods of the road were willing, we'd roll into New York City.

We left the offices we'd been renting in Bulwer Street and got to the corner where we waved to the families we wouldn't see for months. Ten yards further we stopped. Petrol. I'd forgotten to fill the tank, so we had to pull over right away. Then, as I was trying to settle the bike on its side-stand, I dropped it. I remember looking at Ewan. It was the second time I'd dropped the bike that morning and I don't do that, not ever. Was this an omen? Was this the shape of things to come?

'Jesus, Charley.' Ewan was looking pretty pensive. 'Have we overloaded the bikes? I mean, this is perfect tarmac – what're they going to be like when we're in Russia or somewhere really out of the way?'

PART FOUR

17 March – 7 June 2016:

London, England

748 SP

After seeing the ankle surgeon, I spent the next few weeks trying to keep my spirits up by reminding myself that I'd actually achieved quite a lot in my life. I gave myself pep talks, telling myself that there was plenty more I wanted to do. In order to remain positive, I had to put all fears about my leg and D-Day to the back of my mind and focus on getting better.

I'd spent years perfecting my skills on a bike and I was determined they would not be wasted. I recalled how I used to ride my Zephyr out to the Westway from Shepherd's Bush where there's a roundabout underneath the flyover. At that time there were no traffic lights and the speed limit on the roundabout itself was 50mph. I swear to God I'd hit that roundabout and not leave for ages. Round and round, circuit after circuit depending on the traffic, I'd build and build to the point where I could get my knee down and keep it there. It was the first place I learned to do that, and on a big old Kawasaki too. I had no protective knee sliders; just leathers, or more often than not a pair of jeans. I distinctly remember touching down for the very first time and feeling the tarmac rip through my jeans. It was a really stupid thing to do, but I wasn't thinking about how easy it would be to tear my kneecap away. I carried on and got to the point where I could keep it hovering just above the road a la Barry Sheene, back in the day.

I was there for hours – days, when you add them all up – doing lap after lap, and maybe I'd get one decent one but then a car would pull onto the roundabout from the slip road, and I'd have to back off before having another go.

I went back again and again before I sold the Zephyr and bought my first GSX-R 750 which I trashed on that slip road off the M4. After that I bought another GSX-R – the SRAD model this time – in red, black and silver. I trashed that on the way home from work one day after painting and decorating. I was riding with a carpenter who was into classic bikes and we were coming through Camden Town. It was a bitterly cold day but I had a notion to pop a wheelie in second gear just the same. It was a good one, really cool – at least while it lasted. But the wheel came down at an angle and the road was slippery; I lost the front and slammed into this really high kerb and that was the end of another Suzuki.

After that I bought another bike from Roy, a Honda XR600R – the bike that had the mind of its own. I'm serious; it was like Telsche's horse not taking the bridle. If you wanted to get that bike started you had to sneak up from behind otherwise it would see you coming and just shut down. You had to kick-start it of course, so I used to stalk it, literally creep up and jump on, then kick the motor over – all without even putting my bike gear on, because that would be a giveaway. I had to be nonchalant, lull the machine into a false sense of security. Once you'd got it going there was nothing it could do.

That was one of my favourite bikes ever. I remember one of Ewan's children being ill in hospital one time when I visited on that XR. As I headed down the Fulham Road I could see him watching from an upstairs window, looking morose, so to cheer him up I popped a monster second gear wheelie.

Aside from the fact it was such a bugger to start, it was a fantastic bike to ride. Honda made it from 1985 all the way through until 2000, a single cylinder four-stroke that was air-cooled and brilliant off-road. When they finally replaced it, they upgraded the engine and gave the bike an aluminium frame. I kept mine for a while but it wasn't something I could do track days on, and by then I'd really got the bug – so I chopped it in for a Yamaha R1. That was the only sportsbike I've ever bought that actually scared me. I remember the first time I rode it, thinking, 'Wow, this is too big, too powerful…' but within a couple of days I was used to it and the power was fantastic. Blue and white with no steering damper, I rode it daily until Ewan offered me the 748. That Ducati was a hell of a gift, and I kept it right up until the day I came out of my house to go to work one morning and found bits of it all over the pavement. I used to chain it up (both front wheel and back) in this little section of gated ground next to my house in Fulham. I figured it was pretty secure, and it was directly below my bedroom so I ought to be able to hear if anyone tried to nick it. That particular night I heard nothing untoward at all, but when I came out in the morning every piece that could've been stolen had indeed disappeared. All that was left were the wheels and frame still held together by the chain.

I used to ride it to work every day no matter what the weather was doing, and despite the fact it was as close to a balls-out race bike as any 750 can get. I'd strap a cardboard box over the back of the seat and carry brushes and sandpaper, rollers and tins of paint. One day as I rode through Wimbledon the box fell off and brilliant white gloss went splashing all over the tarmac.

I rode that bike down to Kent one freezing winter's weekend, after my friend Philip Knatchbull invited me to his father's house for a pheasant shoot. Most of the guests rolled up in Range Rovers, toting guns and dressed in tweeds. I had tweeds of a sort I suppose, though I looked like a bit of a farmer. I wore them under a set of waterproofs all the way from Fulham with a shotgun slung over my shoulder. When I pulled up on my bike, my hands were so cold that I couldn't uncurl my fingers from the grip position, let alone squeeze the trigger on a 12 bore.

So I had much on my mind, both past and present, as I lay confined in my downstairs bed still unable to put any weight on either foot. I was really pissed off; I had been sure by now I'd be on crutches. The Beckham boot was so uncomfortable I often took it off. I would sleep in it, but during the day I'd let the air get to my foot because my skin was sweating and itchy.

Olly was still tending to my every need, and that included bathing me and wiping my arse. On top of that there was Ziggy who wasn't very well and had to be taken to the vet. To cap it all, we were about to get a panicked phone call from Doone.

It was couple of weeks after my visit to the ankle surgeon. Our eldest daughter was skiing in the Alps with a university group; in fact she had only just got out there having spent 24 hours on a coach. I think she'd managed one full day on the slopes before she called in the early hours of the morning to tell me she'd slipped on a patch of ice. She was very upset and I had to calm her down, wondering why it had taken this long to phone if she'd fallen while she was skiing.

'I wasn't skiing,' she said. 'It was tonight, Dad, in the town. I slipped on a patch of ice on the road and banged my head.'

'Your head?' I was really concerned now. 'Are you OK?'

She was silent for a moment and I wasn't sure if that was for my benefit, but when she spoke again she sounded calmer. 'Yeah, I'm alright, Dad. I'm OK.'

'Are you sure, Doone? What time is it out there?'

'It's alright. Don't worry. Look, I'll call you again in the morning.'

In reality she was anything but alright. I found out later that she'd been messing about with a friend and taken a fall, but she wasn't able to get her hands out to take her weight. She cracked the icy pavement with her chin so hard she was

spitting blood and bits of broken teeth. Luckily the group's
ski guides were with them and they picked her up and took
her to what they call the 'Night Angel'. It's a first aid outpost
in the mountain resort rather than a hospital emergency
room – a necessity as the nearest doctor and hospital was an
hour and a half's drive down the mountain. Patched up a
little, Doone looked in the mirror and saw that one of her
teeth was sticking out horizontally from her gum. That
really freaked her out; she panicked again, terrified. She was
still spitting blood and had a deep gash in her chin – she
really needed a hospital.

But that was impossible. It was freezing cold and the
roads would be covered in ice. The guides told her that to
drive right then would be to invite disaster. There was
nothing they could do until the morning.

I don't think anyone had any idea how bad the injury
actually was. They probably thought the way Doone was
carrying on was down to shock more than anything else.
But it turned out that her jaw was broken and half her teeth
were cracked. She was in a blind panic, but they took her
back to the chalet so she could go to bed. She tried to sleep
but it was impossible with the amount of pain she was in.
Realising she was hungry, she went to the kitchen and
poured a bowl of cereal. It was at that point she found she
couldn't open her mouth properly, and that freaked her out
all over again.

In the morning, she was taken to a doctor who stitched
up her chin. He was so amazed by how deep the cut was that
he called the nurses to come and see. They confirmed she'd

broken her jaw, and then she called me again. To her credit she was really calm and composed by then. She just gave me the facts and we set about trying to get her home. We could barely believe it – the second Boorman medivac in a couple of months. The doctors took the X-rays and gave her painkillers, but she had to go to the hospital. She was there six hours and one of the biggest problems was the language barrier; she couldn't speak enough French to make the nurses understand her and they couldn't speak enough English.

In a lot of pain and worried about how she was going to look with her teeth smashed, all Doone wanted to do was get on a flight and come home. There was one to Gatwick that left at 8.30 that evening and she was determined to be on it. But she still didn't know the full extent of the damage or what would be proposed by way of treatment and they told her she wasn't allowed to leave until she had that information.

Groundhog Day: it was like what had happened to me was happening all over again, only now it was my daughter with acute multiple trauma and I was feeling even more helpless. I couldn't speak enough French to find out exactly what was going on and neither could Olly. In the end we called Katrine in New York. She phoned Doone and, as luck would have it, the consultant Doone had been waiting to see arrived at that moment and Doone was able to pass the phone to her. The consultant explained to Katrine what was going on, and Katrine translated for Doone. To cut a long story short, we arranged a taxi to the airport and Doone was on that evening flight home.

So now there were two of us for Olly to look after – three if you count Ziggy, who was also on tramadol. The very next morning Olly took Doone to the Dental Institute at King's College Hospital that specialises in acute multiple trauma. She'd spoken to a really close friend of hers called Claire who works in the field of dental care, who'd suggested this was the best course of action since the consultant had made it clear that Doone would need extensive dental treatment. At King's they wired her jaw and fitted thick-banded braces to her teeth. She was pretty subdued when she got home and told me it would be soup and mashed potatoes for weeks.

In early April Ewan called to see how I was and I put on a decent enough front, though I was really beginning to sweat on the upcoming appointment with my leg surgeons.

'It buggered up a tour of Tasmania,' I told him. 'And I'm supposed to be in South America in September; though that's not looking likely, even in the support vehicle.'

'What about your plans for the Darien Gap?'

'I'll make it.' I don't know if I was trying to convince him or myself. 'We've had to put it back til March next year, but I'll make it, Ewan. I have to.'

'Good on you, mate,' he said. 'I know it's tough – just keep your chin up, eh?'

After I hung up the phone I wheeled myself through the hall and opened the front door to get a little fresh air, though there were builders renovating next door and the street was pretty noisy. I sat for a moment just thinking…then wheeled myself up the road with the dog trotting beside me. When I say up the road that's what I mean; the actual road, not the pavement. Pavements are so cracked and full of obstacles I have no idea how permanently disabled people deal with them. Making a circuit of the block, I got back to the house and paused by the motorbikes lined up outside the living room window. A Triumph and a retro Kawasaki rat bike I'd built myself, as well as Olly's Vespa moped. That was of particular interest because, as I mentioned before, it doesn't have footpegs – and so would be my first challenge to overcome when the Beckham boot was off and I was able to get about on crutches. In the old days, mopeds had footpegs on either side like a normal motorbike. When I was growing up it was the Yamaha FS1E or 'Fizzy' everyone was riding, but nowadays they all have a foot-well like a scooter where you place your feet. That would make it much easier to ride when the time came because the frame wouldn't get in the way.

But that was still a long way off, and the sense of confinement I was feeling became so bad that I took the Beckham boot off again and began to work the muscles of my ankle. I was sick of being on my butt, unable to do anything for myself – and I had a brand new Range Rover on loan to me, parked on the other side of the road.

Like a long-term convict who can see a hole in the fence, I grabbed the keys and wheeled myself across the road. I had a smile on my face and a delicious sense of anticipation. Opening the door, I worked the wheelchair right to the edge of the kerb then hoisted myself up to the point where

I was bearing weight on the ankle that should still have been encased in the boot. It hurt like hell, but I didn't think it was going to give way and I was on a mission now. Leaving the wheelchair on the pavement, I climbed in, closed the door and started the engine. My God it was gorgeous, sitting up high with a steering wheel in front of me and the throbbing sound of an engine. Checking the mirrors, I tested my right foot on the accelerator pedal and I could work it alright. It seemed to be OK.

Nothing was going to stop me now. I pulled out of the parking space and headed down the road. Jesus, I could not believe it; I felt independent for the first time in months. I made a couple of circuits of the roads close to where we live then drove as far as the river. There were boats making their way up and down, people running along the walkways, and I was jealous of the way they moved with such ease. Discretion finally became the better part of valour though, and I turned the nose of the car around.

'Oh, shit,' I muttered as I closed on the house. 'Someone's taken my parking space.'

There was nowhere to park; the space I'd vacated had been taken, though the wheelchair was exactly where I'd left it. I can only wonder what the driver thought when they saw the chair but I doubt they would have associated it with the empty parking space and missing Range Rover. The only place I could pull in was significantly further up the street from the house.

So there I was, marooned in a parking space miles from my wheelchair, and there was no pedestrian about that I could ask to fetch it. I didn't even have my phone with me so I couldn't call Olly or Doone. I sat there for ages hoping someone would come along but it was a cold spring day in suburban Barnes and the road was deserted. Finally, I resorted to hitting the horn again and again in an attempt to attract the attention of those at home. It took a while, but eventually Olly and Doone came out to see what all the commotion was about and spotted the empty wheelchair. I had the window down and called out from further up the road.

'Hi, guys,' I said. 'Can you fetch the chair for me?'

For a moment, they just stared at me. Then they looked at each other, shaking their heads. 'Dad,' Doone said. 'What the hell are you doing?'

'Thought I'd go for a drive,' I replied, a sheepish smile on my face. 'I just went around the block but someone pinched my space.'

With a shake of her head my long-suffering wife crossed the road and fetched the wheelchair for me.

The following day I went to see Rupert Eckersley for an update on my hand. I really wasn't sure how it was doing, though I was wheeling myself around the house now without any pain. But it still seemed very swollen; I pointed that out, and he told me the progress was exactly as he'd hoped it would be.

'It's looking good, Charley. Don't worry about the swelling – the skin is thicker than it was but that's to be expected, and it might never go back to how it used to be.'

He gave me an encouraging smile. 'It doesn't matter. The range of movement is really good and there's no need for physio, at least not at the moment. The hand will always feel slightly different because we're going to leave the plate where it is unless there are complications.'

He checked my left hand as well. After the accident they had to take my wedding ring off because I'd damaged what's called the 'PIP' joint. It was pretty swollen and again he told me it could take a long time to go down. But his final words were hopeful: 'All in all, your hands are a whole lot better than when I had to fix them the first time.' He was talking about what happened at the Dakar Rally when I came off my bike in a dried-up riverbed, lying in the dirt with the prospect of some massive truck racing down to flatten me.

Between the two global expeditions I made with Ewan, I took on the infamous off-road endurance race from Lisbon in Portugal to the Senegalese capital, Dakar. For as long as I can remember I've wanted to race a motorbike but I'd missed my chance when it came to short circuits or the roads. But I was pretty good at riding off-road and a rally like the Dakar was still an option. The opportunity came in the wake of the success generated by *Long Way Round*. After that I had something to offer TV companies in my own right, plus the Dakar is one of the most dangerous and brutal races on the planet. It's filmed anyway, from crews on the ground as well as in helicopters, and there had to be a way we could use that as well as creating our own footage.

Once again I got together with Russ Malkin and we set about trying to work out how a TV series would play out. We talked to Simon Pavey who runs the BMW Off Road Skills school in South Wales where Ewan and I had trained, because Simon had done the Dakar a bunch of times as well as countless other off-road races. We decided a team effort would be better than just me trying to negotiate the dunes on my own, so we roped him in as well as Matt Hall, an antiques dealer who'd filmed some of the stuff Simon had been involved with in Australia.

It felt like a good fit, the three of us; but to take on the race was a serious risk and I understood that right from the get-go. Every year people died on the Dakar but I was determined I wouldn't be one of them. I spoke to Olly and we weighed up the pitfalls. I wasn't sure how she'd react initially but she was used to me taking chances. I'd been away for four months the last time and there were hairy moments on *Long Way Round* – and not just on the motorbike. Some of the places we wound up at were pretty sketchy, not to mention some of the people.

'Remember Igor, Charley?' Olly said.

Remember? Even though it had been a while since I thought about him, how could I forget? Back in 2004, Ewan and I crossed Europe and were in Ukraine riding in *Long Way Round*. In fact, we'd just been nicked for speeding by a copper called Vladimir close to a town named Krasnyi Luch. We'd managed to get hold of our fixer Sergey and he'd had a word with the copper on our behalf, told him where we were from and what we were doing, and the copper ended up inviting us to spend the night at his house. That was some kind of turn around and the expedition was all about getting to know the people, so we followed him beyond Krasnyi Luch to a place called Antratsyt.

I don't know if he called ahead, but as we pulled into the town square we found a welcoming committee gathered. They seemed to be led by this young Mafioso-looking guy who could've stepped from the set of *The Sopranos*. He was driving a silver BMW M5, the only western car for miles, and rather than stay with Vladimir the cop it transpired we'd been invited to his house instead. His name was Igor and we got the feeling that despite the smiles and photos, the bonhomie, he was not the kind of guy you said 'no' to. Vladimir indicated for us to follow his car, and judging by the way he skipped red lights and cut up all the other vehicles, it seemed that Igor was the head honcho in these parts. He led us through the shabby little town to a set of iron gates and his mansion.

It was massive; I'm not kidding. It was so out of sync with the rest of the place we thought this guy had to be a little hooky. But it was too late to change our minds, and the last thing we wanted to do was offend him. The gates opened and we rode into a kind of compound. Parking the bikes, Ewan and I looked at each other briefly before following Igor up a flight of marble steps into his palatial home. He introduced us to his wife and we checked out the high ceilings as we climbed another flight of stairs. Gesturing for us to walk ahead of him, he took us all the way up to a vast attic room that would house not just Ewan and me, but the whole crew.

'You sleep here,' Igor explained. 'You cannot stay with Vladimir tonight – his wife, she will not allow it.'

Now we understood why the cop had ushered us this way. He'd promised we'd have somewhere to stay and he wasn't going to go back on his word. The room really was enormous, furnished with beds and some easy chairs and a chest of drawers. A few pictures hung on the walls and I did a double-take as my gaze fastened on a machine gun hanging by its strap. I couldn't believe my eyes, and Igor picked up on my surprise. He fetched the gun; a Thompson (Tommy Gun) from the USA. Working the bolt, he held it one-handed like an old-time gangster and now there was no expression on his face at all. 'Partisans,' he said. 'Russian freedom fighters.' Squeezing the trigger, he smiled.

The gun wasn't loaded, thank God, but it wasn't the only one he had. They were everywhere; various different handguns, Kalashnikovs, hunting rifles. Over a rowdy and raucous dinner he told us he'd been a turbine mechanic on the Atlantic submarine patrols at the height of the Cold War. We figured that now he was into a whole other business altogether, and that suspicion was confirmed when halfway through dinner the doorbell rang and a heavyset man came in. He had the scarred, callused hands of a bare-knuckle fighter and one low-slung sleepy eye. As he shook hands with Ewan he just about crushed his fingers. He said something in Ukrainian to Igor then opened his jacket, took a pistol from a shoulder holster and laid it down on the table. Ewan looked across at me, his expression plain to read: what the fuck are we doing in this house?

'Yes, I remember Igor,' I said to Olly. The Dakar? It held no fear.

DRIP, DRIP, DRIP

That's not true, it held plenty of fears. It's a race through the desert and if you're not a little nervous each morning before you set off on a stage then you're a fool. I've seen riders on the grid at the MotoGP take so many piss breaks before they head out on the warm-up lap that they might as well have brought a pee bottle. James Hunt used to throw up before every Formula 1 Grand Prix.

When the time came for me to line up with the other competitors at the Dakar starting line, I was aware of this drip, drip, drip of unease. I'd had it pretty much since we made the decision to race, a little chill that was perpetually there. Fear is a good thing: it keeps us on our toes, and I remember Simon Pavey telling me that in order to feel truly alive you need to scare yourself a little every day.

When you ride a motorbike the risk is always there. You're exposed, vulnerable to the elements and other road users in a way that you just don't experience in a car. If somebody hits you when you're on a motorbike you are going to get hurt. It's your body that takes the impact and not the wing or door of the car. Sometimes you get on your bike and just make it dance. Other days you're so wooden and wobbly, you think you can't ride to save your life. You still do it though, because riding a bike gives you a rush you just can't get anywhere else. When you're clicking through the gears, accelerating hard or peeling into a tight bend, the feeling is awesome but a hint of fear is always there.

Laid up with my bones broken as a result of chasing that feeling, I was experiencing that same dripping sense of unease that I'd felt throughout the Dakar Rally. I was in another race; a different kind of race where each waypoint, each mark on the map, was the next surgical consultation.

Every day of planning for the Dakar, that drip, drip, drip was there. I knew what I was taking on and although there was a sense of excitement as we set up a deal for the bikes, there was still this underlying sense of fear. I knew the enormity of the task and how the race could so easily be the end of me. It was different to anything I'd done before. The trip with Ewan had its difficulties but this was a whole new ball game. The only time I was free of that sensation was when I was actually on the bike in the middle of each stage. You don't have time to be scared when you're on the bike – you're too busy trying to keep the bubble up and rubber down. But as soon as the stage was done the unease returned.

My dad talked about something similar, a sense of trepidation every time he took on the challenge of making another movie. He's often said that movies gave him his life but they took it from him as well. Nothing is ever really achieved without cost. I could see it in him, feel it, as I grew up. Locations, difficult actors, producers and budgets, the studio hammering away at him. Everything seemed to conspire against him being successful but he never shirked the challenge. 'Don't do anything by halves, Charley,' I remember him telling me. 'If you're going for it, go all the way.'

That creeping sensation, that feeling of dread; I'd been aware of it the night before my Dakar Race ended in Morocco, just three days into the African stage. The road book had been bothering me and I couldn't quite get to grips with it; a rolling paper map that's fixed on the motorbike's dash which the rider uses to find the obstacles along the route of each stage. You're on your own out there. There's no navigator on a bike as there is in a car rally. The road book is your only source of navigation and you have to be able to figure it out, navigate and ride at the same time, which is fairly dangerous. It's easy to make a mistake and end up going the wrong way. If you crash or break down you're liable to be hit by a car.

The bike I was using was a BMW F650RR that had been built specifically for me and was much lighter than the R1150GS I'd ridden on *Long Way Round*, but still heavier than some of the other bikes in the race. BMW supplied us with an original that we sent to Nick Plumb, the owner of Touratech UK. That's a German company with a UK facility near Swansea that specialises in modifying bikes for off-road expeditions. They made the panniers that saved Ewan's life when he was hit by a car on the final, seemingly innocuous leg of *Long Way Round*.

In order to get the bike exactly right we drew on Simon Pavey's existing experience and came up with a machine that was designed to negotiate most (if not all) of the pitfalls he had come across before. Apart from the regular upgrades to brakes and suspension, we had all manner of spare parts hidden away in various cubby-holes. We carried new gear levers and clutch plates inside an aluminium side-casing that had been designed so we could change the clutch without having to remove the water pump. We also switched all the bolts to one-size-fits-all instead of the array of different sizes that meant carrying a much larger and heavier set of tools.

We were three days in, and I'd embarked on that race as ready as any novice could be. Things had gone pretty well. We finished the second stage and, dog-tired, we spent the night at a place called Ouarzazate. Tomorrow would be the longest stage so far and that was a little daunting. We'd completed more than 3,000 kilometres since we began in Portugal, just over a third of the race distance, and I was feeling much better than I had at the start. Three days without a serious incident; the dripping sensation was still with me but it wasn't quite as deep-seated as it had been. I'm never one for tempting fate though, and the following day I'd be looking at another 819 kilometres to get to Tan-Tan, so nothing could be taken for granted.

Up long before it was light, I was off around 5am with 187 kilometres of tarmac to negotiate before the stage actually began. That was the pattern with the Dakar; every morning we had miles of road to ride before the stage even got going. That day we had 350 kilometres of 'special section' to negotiate, which was a pretty ugly-looking prospect. Wadis (ravines) and chotts (lakes and marshes) were littered here and there, though at this time of the year they ought to be dry. I'd also be riding the dunes; smooth, loose sand and potentially the most dangerous terrain. I knew them only too well – while practicing in Dubai, I'd come off the bike in the dunes and broken my collarbone. With fewer obvious obstacles the temptation is to really go for it and the chances of a spill are that much higher.

I was up for it even if I was cold. The nights in the desert are freezing and I set out with a bin bag tied over my jacket to try and keep out the worst of the wind. Thank God my BMW had been fitted with hand warmers because if my fingers had frozen I don't know how I would've coped. I was up front with Simon and Matt following; as three members of the same team our race numbers were 172, 173, and 174.

I can't tell you what that felt like. I mean, to actually have a race number. I'd wanted a genuine, bona fide race number since the first time I ever took part in a track day. Remember what I said about feeling like I'd missed my vocation? Well, when I was sitting on my bike at the start of the Dakar with a race number on my back, I was on a podium above a massive crowd with Simon on my left and Matt on my right. The race announcer was calling out our names, the crowd was cheering, and I was high on the buzz of adrenalin. A novice about to start the most dangerous race in the world, I remember gazing over all those people and thinking I could win this. Moments later I almost lost the front coming down the slope and narrowly avoided ending up on my arse. Catching it just before it went over, I quickly decided that just finishing the race would be OK.

For a long time now it's occurred to me that just making the start of any venture is success in itself. I had made the start. I had a race number. I was a novice for sure, but I was riding with Simon and he'd competed in lots of enduros. Originally from Australia, by the time he was 19 he was racing six-day events in French Polynesia then competing professionally in Japan. He told me that whenever he won, the team owners would pat him on the back because winning was his job. If he came second or third, nobody in the team would speak to him.

I remember one night we were sitting around talking about our experiences and someone brought up the 'Finke'. The Tatts Finke Desert Race is known as the fastest desert race in Australia, and is one of the most difficult and remote courses in the world. Starting out of Alice Springs, a single line of cars, bikes, quads and buggies race to the Finke river and back. It takes place every year on the Queen's Birthday weekend, and Simon stopped us in our tracks when he told us he held the world record.

'For the Finke?' I said. 'You've got to be kidding.'

'No, Charley, straight up. I hold the world record for the Finke.'

'Jesus, I had no idea.'

'For the fastest ever airlift to hospital,' he added. 'I think I made about 400 yards before I crashed and they had to get me out of there.'

As it got light that morning a pretty strong wind was blowing and we just knew the dust would be a bitch. It was. All day the wind blew from the southwest and we had to negotiate the stage in a constant haze. Every now and again the gloom was penetrated by a helicopter that would pop up from below the horizon. The chopper was something of a mixed blessing; since it was carrying the cameras we were relying on, when it was there at least you knew you were reading the road book right and hadn't missed any navigation points. The downside was the rotor creating sheets of dust. Not that it really mattered that day; the dust had been in our faces since we set out.

As the chopper appeared, Matt came racing past. We were at the foot of a really steep climb and I guess he wanted the cameraman to follow him as he stood on the pegs with his elbows out like a pro. The chopper didn't follow him though – it stayed with me. Maybe the cameraman could see I wasn't having such a good time and there might be some drama ahead. I was really pissed off because I was finding the section tough as shit and Matt seemed to be just flying. The hill was a ten-mile climb and it seemed to go on and on. Already he was way ahead, negotiating the track with ease whereas I had all sorts of demons rushing about in my head. It wasn't the dread anymore, it was a sour feeling that this had been a really bad idea from the get-go and I wasn't up to it after all. I kept hitting rocks and bouncing off with the front end jagging so badly I almost lost it. My feet were slipping off the pegs and all I wanted to do was pack it in, get on a plane and go home.

But then, in my mind's eye, I saw my dad. I heard him bitching about what the Hollywood studios were telling him to do and how he was going to make the movie he wanted. I saw him with his eye to the lens of a viewfinder, waist-deep in the Amazon River, and I told myself to 'man up' and kicked into gear.

I reminded myself that I was just as good a hill climber as Matt. The mistake I was making was target fixation. I thought about all I'd learned down the years and how this was no different to taking a corner. My field of vision was too close. I wasn't looking far enough ahead. Look ahead and you see the obstacles long before you get to them. Do that and you have time to manoeuvre around them, and they're no longer obstacles. I told myself to chill a little; I could do this. I was a racer with a race number and it was time to show that cameraman just what I could do.

I made it to the top of the hill and rode down the other side with much more confidence. I was skipping along, so much so I actually passed Matt on the way. I stopped where the road forked to check the book on my dash and he came up alongside.

'It's this way, Charley,' he called, veering sideways.

I saw the line he was taking and it looked to be OK. *Alright,* I thought, *he seems to know where he's going.* So I set off after him.

It became apparent pretty quickly that this route wasn't what was in the road book. I could see that, and it wasn't long before Matt must've realised it too. He pulled up, shaking his head. 'Wrong way,' he said. 'Sorry, Charley. We've taken the wrong track. We missed the waypoint.'

We turned back the way we had come, thinking that Simon had to be somewhere on the trail behind us. We hadn't seen him all day and thought we'd run into him as we turned back. Since we'd missed the waypoint we decided the sensible thing to do was go back to the last actual checkpoint. We did that and had our time cards stamped so we wouldn't incur a penalty, and asked the officials if they'd seen Simon. They told us he had been through already and was now some distance ahead. I was a little bit surprised by that because he'd been well behind – but then again he was the pro, and Matt and I the novices.

We rode on through the morning and into the afternoon as the landscape alternated between loose sand, rock-strewn tracks and sections of coarse camel grass. Riding in the afternoon was far more dangerous than the morning because by then the cars and trucks had caught up and they would come rattling through at speed. Most of the time they literally forced us out of the way. They left great clouds of dust in their wake and we'd be so blinded we had no choice but to pull up.

That meant a lot of stopping and starting, and that was a nightmare. Off-road riding is all about rhythm and ours was continually broken. Matt had been off his bike already when a fast car forced him to the side and he hit a rock. Not long after that I had my own close call when another car was right on my arse with the driver hitting his sentinel way too late to tell me he was there. The sentinel was the alarm every bike and car carried to let other competitors know a vehicle was approaching and that day mine was ringing out like a death knell. That last one was the closest call I'd had, and my heart was hammering away. I was tired, really knackered; we'd been riding since 5am and, with the trucks upon us, any slip in reaction time could be fatal.

We rode on and after another 70 kilometres we stopped at the second checkpoint to refuel the bikes. Again, we were told that Simon had long since been through and we were still a little surprised. We set off after him. Feeling refreshed from the short break, I was enjoying myself now. I was riding to about 80 per cent of my ability because any more and I'd have nothing in reserve. That's the way to stay safe: you have to give yourself somewhere to go. Ride within your limits and that enables you to react quickly when you have to.

A few kilometres later I came up on a serious wadi. The road book was telling me not to go directly across, but to make my way around a bloody great hump then descend to the riverbed below. I was a little confused because I could see a clear track that ran right by the hump and it looked alright to me. But the road book is the road book; it's your bible when you're out there, so I changed down a gear or two, preparing to go around the hump – just as this massive KAMAZ truck came thundering past. The driver didn't avoid the hump, and he barely avoided me. I watched as he took the straightest track and I thought, *Fuck it, that's got to be the way to go.*

Mistake, Charley: stick to the road book. Too late. Without warning my front wheel just stepped sideways. The bike went over and I was on my side with my helmet filling with gravel. I was in a slide, still hooked to the bike and the stones scraping the side of my face. *What the fuck?* I thought. *What the hell happened? How did I lose the front?*

I came to a stop with the bike on top of me. At various stages throughout the race I'd wished for the much lighter, nimbler KTM, but never so much as then. The BMW was lying across my leg and it weighed almost a quarter of a ton. Half on my back, half on my side, I tried to lift it clear – and this white-hot pain seared through both my hands. I was literally screaming. There was no way I could get the bike off my legs and all I could think about was that KAMAZ just now and how another could be along any time. I started to panic, lying in the dirt at the bottom of a dried-up river with God knows how many cars and trucks rushing up behind me. The worst of it was knowing they would be going too fast to avoid me. If I got hit now I would see it coming, and that thought filled me with a sense of terror I'd never encountered before.

Thank God I wasn't on my own. Matt was there behind me and as he pulled up I was shouting at him to get the bike off me and get me up. My mouth was full of sand and gravel and I could barely get the words out.

'Get me up, Matt, before a car comes!'

Fortunately another rider had also stopped, and he stood watch while Matt dragged the bike off my legs.

My hands were in agony; they were so painful I could hardly focus to get to my feet. Already my right hand seemed so swollen that the flesh filled up my glove. When I tried to move my fingers I nearly passed out. I could feel bones literally grinding against each other and I almost threw up. I bent double, retching, though there was nothing to bring up. My head swam, I was dizzy; I almost fell over again.

My left hand was no better. The thumb hurt like hell, worse than my right and it was so far out of shape that even with the glove on I could see it was pointing the wrong way. I don't know how I managed it, but I got back on the bike and rode another 400 kilometres to Tan-Tan where the doctor told me my hands were smashed and my race to Dakar was over.

I had too much time to think. Reliving that crash again wasn't doing me any good; I could almost hear that drip, drip, drip in my head. It wasn't the only sound I could hear, though. As if all my contemplation had triggered something, I grew aware of a sort of clicking sound when I moved my index finger. At first I thought I was imagining it; but I wasn't, it was there alright, a real metallic kind of click whenever I moved my finger.

'Olly,' I called. 'Olivia?'

'What is it?' She appeared in the living room doorway.

'My hand...there's something wrong with my hand, the screw holding the plate in place at the knuckle. I can feel it moving. I think it's come loose.'

As if I didn't have enough appointments to cope with, I was back with the hand surgeon just a few days after seeing him the last time. He took a look and confirmed that I hadn't imagined the clicking, but the wound was what he called 'quiet'. It didn't sound quiet to me, but he said that was the technical term for nothing untoward going on. What I could hear was crepitus. I had no idea what that meant, and he explained that it was the grating sound or sensation you get between bone and cartilage or the fractured parts of a bone when muscles are moved. That was sound I had heard when I got the bike off my legs during the Dakar, but he told me this was cartilage sliding across the plated site of the fracture.

He took an X-ray and didn't find anything that hadn't been there the last time he saw me, so all was OK. On the way home Olly suggested that I was edgy and more nervous than usual, perhaps because the date of the really important consultation was getting closer by the day. I tried to tell myself it wasn't that at all, that I'm a guy whose glass is always three-quarters full and I wasn't worrying – but deep down I knew she was right.

Fortunately, I had a distraction. Since *Long Way Round* hit the screens I've done a lot of work for the Duke of Edinburgh Scheme and one of my roles is to hand out the Gold Awards at St James's Palace. I was due at Buckingham Palace this year for the 60th anniversary of the award, and was looking forward to it despite being confined to a wheelchair.

The day arrived and all the ambassadors were there, with some 700 people gathered in the palace garden. Olly pushed me in the wheelchair with the frame on my left leg and the Beckham boot on the right. The men were all in suits, the women in dresses and hats, all of them except me. I was sort of makeshift really; a shirt and jacket covering the top half of my body and a pair of shorts below. The frame was so awkward it meant I couldn't wear trousers. I'd been in shorts since I came home from the hospital and I was wearing them again that day. I handed out the awards as I always did and the recipients wanted photos. They asked if I could stand up so I could be in the pictures with them and I just about managed that, resting my weight on the foot that was still encased in the Beckham boot. I was in just that position when the Duke of Edinburgh headed our way. He looked at my jacket and tie, then he looked down at the shorts and my incapacitated legs. Raising an eyebrow, he passed on by.

That wasn't the first time I'd been underdressed in the company of royalty – though how I came to be so the first time around is part of a much longer story.

I got involved with the Movember Foundation in 2010, after my wife took the dog to the vet. It was just a regular check-up for Ziggy and everything was going fine. That was until the last examination, when the vet took a good look at the poor spaniel's testicles. Feeling something odd, he had a closer look and he could see that one of them was slightly misshapen.

'We need to check that,' he said. 'It doesn't look right. I think we should look a little more closely.'

Olly took a look herself now and a frown spread across her brows. 'Charley's got a testicle like that,' she said. 'The right one, it looks just like that.'

'What?' The vet stared at her.

'My husband – one of his testicles is just like that.'

'Olivia,' his demeanour had suddenly changed. 'When you get home you need to make sure he goes to see the doctor right away.'

As soon as she got home Olly told me what had happened and what the vet had said. She told me I needed to go to the doctor, and quickly, and then she picked up the phone. I was stunned, not quite taking in what she'd been saying or the implications of what it could mean.

The next morning, however, I was in the GP's surgery peeling off my underwear, about to be subjected to the first of what would turn out to be many intimate inspections of my testicles by an endless parade of doctors. The doctor examined me thoroughly, and his expression was a little grim. 'Charley,' he said. 'There's something not right here. I'm going to refer you to the consultant for an ultrasound scan. You need to make the appointment as soon as you get home.'

I told him I would do that, and he gave me the details and said he would inform the hospital immediately to expect my call.

I have to admit I was pretty freaked out. But in a stereotypically male fashion, I suppose, by the time I got home I'd calmed down a bit and procrastinated, put off making that important call right away. I left it, and I might've left it longer if the phone hadn't rung at 7.45am the following day with my GP on the end of the line. He had never done that. In 20 years he'd never rung me at home before.

'Charley,' he said. 'Did you make the appointment like I said? The ultrasound at the hospital – did you make the call?'

'No,' I said. 'I didn't, not yet. I…'

'Do it now. Do it as soon as you put down the phone.'

Now I was really worried. No one had actually used the word cancer, but that's what was at the back of my mind. It brought back memories of my sister Telsche and all that had happened to her. Needless to say, I got on the phone right away – and within a week I was sitting in the consultant's office at the hospital as he examined me just as the GP had done. His face carried the same serious expression as he sent me to have the ultrasound. It wasn't very long before I was told I had testicular cancer.

I can't explain what it feels like to have a doctor tell you something like that. Just the word 'cancer' alone is enough to shake your emotional foundations; and I had so many memories of my sister's fight with the illness, which she eventually lost. The consultant was aware of the family history and he was at pains to tell me this was nothing like what had happened to Telsche. He described it as an inconvenience, not something that was going to radically change my life.

It didn't matter what he said. Being told you've got any cancer is life-changing. You sit there with this ticking time bomb inside you and all you want to do is get it out. In my case that was immediate. The surgery was booked pretty much there and then. They would remove the cancerous testicle and the consultant asked me if I wanted a prosthetic one in its place.

'What?' I said, peering across the desk. 'What do you mean?'

'We're taking a testicle out and that's going to feel very different. We can fit you with a false one if you like, so you'll feel more normal, more balanced so to speak.'

A little unsure, I turned to my wife. 'What do you think, Olly?' I said.

'Fine with me, just as long as it's bigger than the last one.'

Within a week I was on a bed waiting for the anaesthetist to put me under when the surgeon came through from theatre with his marker pen to make sure everyone knew just which testicle they were going to remove.

'You know what,' I said as he prepared to make his mark. 'I think I should be the one to mark it – just in case.'

With a nod, he handed me the pen. Then he stood back with his arms folded across his chest. 'You sure about that, Charley? Are you sure you'll mark the right one? What if you make a mistake – you are dyslexic, after all.'

I was poised with the pen in mid-air looking down on my private parts.

'Alright,' I said, 'since you put it like that. I suppose you'd better do it – but make sure you get it right.'

He duly marked the spot and put the pen aside, a smile on his face. His parting shot was to pop a finger in his cheek. 'Easy as shelling peas; nothing to it really. You'll be fine.'

The operation went ahead and I woke up with that image of someone shelling peas rolling around in my head. Before the surgery was booked I'd asked the consultant if there would be any, you know, side effects, long term or otherwise; but he assured me everything would work as it had before. Of course, I didn't totally believe him and I could think about nothing else that night after the surgery as they kept me in for observation. Finally I fell asleep, but when Olly arrived in the morning I had the biggest smile on my face. 'Guess what,' I said. 'When I woke up this morning the sheets looked like a Bedouin tent.'

The surgery was successful. They told me they'd got every bit of the cancerous tissue out and I had a session of chemotherapy about a month later. As they administered the drip they explained that it would weaken me quite a bit so I had to make sure I had nothing strenuous planned for at least a day or two. I told them I understood. What I didn't tell them was that I had a track day lined up with Ron Haslam at Donington Park in the morning. I hate missing track days and I was buggered if I was missing this one. The doctors gave me some pills to take if I felt really weak or queasy and I figured that would be OK. Sticking them in a pocket, I headed up the motorway early the following day.

By lunchtime I was feeling weak as a kitten and so bilious I almost threw up. Pulling into pit lane after a couple of flying laps I took my helmet off and the instructor looked at me as if he'd seen a ghost.

'Jesus, you're pale, Charley. Are you alright?'

'I feel bit sick actually. I've got some pills I really ought to take.'

'Why?' he said. 'Have you got a bug or something?'

I shook my head. 'No, nothing like that. I had chemo yesterday. They said it would take it out of me a bit.'

He stared at me with his eyes popping out of his head. 'Chemo, as in chemotherapy…is that what you mean?'

I nodded. 'Yeah,' I said. 'I had testicular cancer but I'm alright now.'

I probably shouldn't have ridden that day but that's just the way I am. It all happened six years ago and I've been clear ever since. The guys from the Movember Foundation read about Olly and the episode with the dog and got in contact, asking if I would tell the story to their members. I did that, in a draughty church hall where about 800 people listened to me telling them how lucky I was to have a wife who was so intimate with my testicles.

Seriously, I cannot stress how important it is to have someone check your testicles at least once every couple of weeks. Whether it's your wife or girlfriend, your boyfriend or husband, a regular physical examination is vital and yet it's something so many men avoid. Think of it this way: you can get naked with your partner, have a bit of a medical examination for a few minutes and, well, what might be a chore or a little embarrassing at first can easily turn into a really good time. If I hadn't had Olly taking such an interest my cancer might have gone undetected, and you know how that can turn out.

Since then I've been involved with Movember, and it's unlike any other charity I've ever come across. Specifically targeting men's health and wellbeing, historically their primary concern has been the prevention of prostrate and testicular cancer. Now, however, they are concentrating as much on men's mental health, particularly because of the high rate of suicide.

Every November awareness is raised by as many men in the UK as possible showing support by growing a moustache all month long. They've raised nearly £500 million since the organisation was founded back in 2003. Along the way there have been plenty of parties and having a good time; it's a real opportunity for getting a bunch of lads together to talk about the kind of stuff men don't usually talk about.

I had to wear a suit to one of the 'Meat-Fest' dinners, where charity members get together in a restaurant for a social gathering. It's an opportunity to meet people who might want to get involved, a sort of male-bonding occasion. We had to bring the wine, and nobody was allowed to show up with a bottle younger than 1984.

Anyway, the suit. I only had one, and it being a Movember do and the weekend, I got absolutely smashed and don't remember leaving the venue or getting home.

I had Sunday to recover but I needed my suit for a Duke of Edinburgh awards ceremony at Buckingham Palace on the Monday. When I woke up on Sunday I checked to see what state it was in, and all I could find were the trousers. There was no sign of the jacket anywhere; I hunted high and low and then realised I must've left it behind at the

Movember event's north London venue. I tried calling but they were closed and weren't going to open again until Monday. I called JC, one of the four founding members of the charity, and told him I had to get my jacket for Monday morning because I was due at the palace. He told me he would be on a plane on Monday and couldn't get to the venue to fetch it.

I didn't know what to do. There wasn't time for me to get up there and be at the palace as well. Jason told me not to worry, and first thing Monday he was on the phone to a taxi company to get someone to collect the jacket and bring it to where I was waiting at the gates of Buckingham Palace. I know what you're thinking – only Charley could be in that sort of situation – and you're probably right. There I was in my shirt and trousers, hopping from one foot to the other, waiting for a taxi to arrive while the guards in their bearskins looked on. In the nick of time a cab arrived and I was slipping my arms through the sleeves of my slightly soiled jacket as I ran to the steps where the ceremony was about to begin.

OLD FRIENDS

As April dragged towards May, it was a round-robin of medical consultations at St Mary's Lindo Wing. Every time I went it was the same procedure: X-ray at 12:30 then across the road for an appointment with my orthopaedic or plastic surgeon. And, of course, I still had multiple injuries being dealt with by different specialists, so no sooner had I seen Eckersley about my hand than I was back at the ankle surgeon's office again.

By late April, my ankle was looking great. There was still quite a bit of swelling and muscle wasting around the shin and calf, but that was to be expected. The pin wound had healed properly and there was no indication of what he called 'neurovascular deficit'.

The best news was the crutches. The surgeon told me it was time to start putting some weight on the right ankle even though I wasn't allowed to put very much on the left. He said I'd still need to wear the boot, but with a pair of crutches I could finally try to get around without the wheelchair, which was a major breakthrough. He also told me it was time for some physiotherapy and referred me to one Pippa Rollitt in Rosslyn Park. He scheduled another appointment with him in six weeks' time and by then I should know if the other leg was healing properly or not.

They issued me with a pair of NHS crutches and finally I could shuffle around. It was fantastic, after months of being on the commode I could go to the loo by myself. Unless you've been in this situation you have no idea how good that makes you feel; at last you get your most intimate, personal moments back to yourself.

Actually, when I was still wheelchair-bound I'd been so fed up with bedpans and the commode that I'd already made it to the toilet, albeit only once. I worked out that if I got the wheelchair to the foot of the stairs I could move from the chair to the lowest step, and then bum shuffle my way along the hall to the toilet door and negotiate the two downward steps. After all, I'd managed to make my way up that set of stone steps outside the ankle specialist's surgery so I was pretty convinced I could make it down the two that led to the sanctuary of the tiny loo. Stupidly perhaps, I decided I'd be able to stand up long enough to be able to sit on the seat and do the business.

So I tried to make it happen, and the first part went off alright. I got from the chair to the stairs and shuffled across the hallway floor. At the toilet door, I worked myself around so I had my back to the loo itself. That's when I discovered that going down a set of steps is actually harder on your bum than going up. I ended up wedged between the toilet and the wall. I couldn't get up. I couldn't move. I was stuck. But I saw the funny side, and was laughing as Kinvara walked past and asked me what the fuck I thought I was doing.

'Kinvara, I'm trying to take a shit,' I said. 'That's what I'm doing.'

She left with a tsk of her tongue and a shake of her head and I summoned the strength to try a second time. Working myself around I shuffled onto the steps and from there I was able to reach for the bowl of the toilet itself. Somehow I made it. The first time I'd been on the loo in months; I could've sat there forever. And I might have had to because I hadn't given a thought to how I'd wipe my arse.

When I got home from the surgeon's office I finally had a bit of freedom. Using the crutches I could hobble across to the kitchen and fetch something from the fridge. I could plug the kettle in and make a cup of tea, and I learned to cover the mug with a piece of cling film so I could carry it back to the couch without spilling it all on the way.

I was supposed to keep the boot on for a while yet, but it was so uncomfortable I took it off early. I was getting about without too much pain and the physio had started with massages on my leg. After a week or so the crutches they'd given me were shelved in favour of a pair I bought myself. The NHS ones had cylindrical handles that chafed so much they cut my hands. The other pair had handles that were shaped to better fit the palm, and I've been using them for months with no chafing at all.

I found them in a mobility shop not far from where we live, the same place that Olivia bought the wheelchair and commode. Meantime I'd been told that a Zimmer frame would be useful so I set about locating one. I bought it on Amazon – and I think this would be a good time to point out how dangerous online shopping can be to someone who's laid up for months.

I found a frame without wheels on the back legs, as recommended, and waited eagerly for it to arrive. It didn't take very long and when the delivery guy rang the doorbell I was across the floor as quickly as the pair of newly acquired crutches would allow. The parcel didn't look very big. That puzzled me so I asked the guy if he'd got the right house. He took a moment to consider the electronic slip.

'Boorman,' he said. 'Charley – that's you, right?'

I nodded. 'Yes, it is.'

'Then this is for you.' He placed the box inside the door and asked me to sign. He was right; it was my name on the label and he had the correct address. Sitting down on the bottom of the stairs I took a knife to the packaging and got it all undone. It was a Zimmer alright, but a child-sized frame; I'd ordered the wrong fucking one.

The Exogen machine my surgeon had recommended arrived the day Ewan, Russ and David came over for lunch. The old crew back together again; a lot had of time had passed and a lot had happened since *Long Way Down*. Russ and I had put together a few TV shows and I'd built up my tour business with Billy. Ewan had concentrated on his Hollywood career. David had a young child now and was developing property in London.

The four of us had a great laugh, though much of the conversation revolved around broken legs. I asked Ewan if he remembered how he'd busted his, the day before our families were due to go skiing.

Of course he remembered. Back in February 2007 he'd been on his way home from the warehouse we'd rented in Avonmore Road to prepare for *Long Way Down*. He was riding one of his older bikes, a BSA Lightning. Produced in Small Heath, Birmingham, between 1965 and 1972, it was the all-round sportsbike of the 1960s: 52 horsepower and capable of just over 110mph. It was one of those bikes they talk about when they refer to the days of mods and rockers and the 'ton-up' club. It came with a close ratio gearbox and high lift camshaft which gave it sportsbike performance without detracting from the Spitfire, which was BSA's balls-out model at the time. The real problem with the Lightning was vibration; it used to rattle away above 5000rpm and you had to slip the clutch under 10mph because the gearing was too high in 1st. From 1969 onwards they made a lot of improvements, widening the crank case and balancing the exhaust pipes, but there was still the problem of too much vibration.

Ewan and I had been away on holiday before and we knew taking a few days would be a great way to catch up before we set off on *Long Way Down*. Time together was what those bike trips were all about; the friendship, the camaraderie that enables us to overcome whatever the road throws at us. I've missed that. Riding with guests is one thing but riding with your buddy is different.

The great thing about old friends and motorbikes is the craic. It's there just as it always was the moment you get together, no matter how much time has passed. In 2014 I was invited on a ten-day biking trip to the Sea of Cortez in the Baja peninsula, Mexico, by 'Eagle Rider' – a company we dealt with when we were doing the *Extreme Frontiers* TV series. I called Jason Connery, who'd been having some family issues, and suggested a bike trip with an old mate would do him good. I was riding an Indian and Jason a Harley and we had a wonderful time. I could not count the years since we'd spent any time on motorbikes together. We'd ride and stop, eat and drink, but mostly just hang out.

Every day we'd wake up with a hangover and decide we weren't going to drink that day. We'd ride until sunset then have a beer or a glass of wine with dinner, then one would turn into two and things would go downhill from there. The war stories would break out and I remember regaling him with one about an awards dinner for the *Top Gear* magazine at a restaurant in Soho. I was at Jeremy Clarkson's table with James May and Richard Hammond, both of whom I've known for years. I'd never been invited to take part as the 'star in a reasonably priced car' and with Clarkson sitting next to me, and the fact we were all pretty drunk, I decided to find out why.

'Am I not a big enough star, Jeremy?' I said. 'Now you're hanging out with the likes of Cruise and Cameron Diaz?'

'Charley,' he said, his eyes a little hooded and his voice beginning to slur. 'It's not that at all.'

'So what is it then?'

'Well, if you don't know I'll tell you.' Elbows on the table, he reached for another bottle of wine. 'The fact is you ride a motorbike and I hate motorbikes. Not only that, you wear leather. Need I say more? Sorry, Charley, you're not coming on my show.'

Anyway, back to the point – that day in February before *Long Way Down*, the Friday night before we were supposed to be skiing in the Alps. We were due to fly out on the Saturday and we'd been working on the bikes at the warehouse, changing the suspension out for Öhlins. There was a buzz about the place now the clock was ticking; everyone was beginning to get excited. Ewan's old R1150GS from *Long Way Round* had been brought to the warehouse and was displayed next to a tough-looking mannequin wearing a Mongolian warrior costume that we'd bid for at a charity auction. February hadn't been the best month for Ewan; he'd had a mole removed from his face after a hint of skin cancer had been detected, then he'd been ill on a hostile training exercise, and was really looking forward to some mountain air.

He stayed pretty late, well into rush hour, and by the time he left the warehouse the roads in west London were heaving. On Holland Road the traffic was at a standstill and Ewan was filtering through the lanes when this guy just stepped from between the vehicles.

Ewan had nowhere to go. Instinct kicked in and he grabbed both brake and clutch and was suddenly into a skid.

He was yelling at the guy to watch out, but the pedestrian just didn't see the bike bearing down on him. Ewan couldn't believe it; he knew that if the bike hit the guy it could kill him, and somehow he managed to chuck the BSA away. He forced it to his right while he peeled off the other way, so it was him not the bike that clattered into the pedestrian. Ewan hit the deck, but the bike seemed to bounce on its back wheel and then it was on top of him. It's a weighty piece of kit and it slammed right into his leg.

For a moment, he just lay there. He was looking up at this guy he'd collided with who was on his feet still and looking down at Ewan with his eyes popping out of his head. Whether he recognised him or not we never found out; Ewan told me later he seemed to be in some kind of stupor.

'Jesus,' Ewan said. 'Are you alright?'

Still the guy just stood there.

'Are you alright?'

'Yeah, I'm fine.' Despite the words he just seemed to hang there.

The bike had Ewan pinned to the ground; he couldn't get the crushing weight off his leg. He spoke to the dumbfounded young man again. 'Can you help me get up?'

'What?' The guy still didn't seem to have any cognisant thought going on, he stood there with his mouth open and his eyes on stalks.

By now lots of people had stopped, and one man came over and carefully lifted the bike off Ewan's leg. He could feel something was wrong and knew he was in trouble.

Somehow he got to his feet, though his right leg didn't feel as if it could take much weight. Sweat in his eyes, he hobbled to a set of steps leading up to a townhouse and sat down. The bike was still running. The guy who had lifted it had managed to get it onto its centre stand, but he couldn't find the key to switch it off because it's not in an obvious position. In the end Ewan had to get up and drag himself across the pavement and do it himself.

Back on the steps he managed to take off his boot and could see he'd grazed his leg pretty badly, but he couldn't make out anything else. He could feel a burning sensation though, and there was a weird feeling just above his ankle. Something didn't feel natural, something wasn't right, and with a ski trip in the morning and the expedition just around the corner, that really worried him.

He tried to keep calm, telling himself it couldn't be a break because if his leg was broken he wouldn't be able to walk. He tried to convince himself of the logic of that and that it had to be just a bad sprain, but when the guy he'd hit came over and asked if he was alright his fears just tumbled out. Ewan said he didn't know if he was alright or not; he thought he might've broken his leg.

'Man, I'm sorry,' the guy said. 'I was looking the other way – it's so noisy out here I didn't hear you and I didn't see you til it was too late.'

'Don't worry about it,' Ewan told him. 'It's not your fault, an accident, just one of those things.'

A female police officer showed up on a horse, and the man whose steps Ewan was sitting on came out of the house and asked if he wanted a cup of tea. Ewan thanked him but shook his head. All he wanted to do was get home. The police woman offered to call an ambulance but he didn't want to go to Casualty – he wanted to get back on his bike.

That's exactly what he did. He had to be in shock because there's no way he'd have been able to do it otherwise. Somehow he managed to pull his boot on, start his bike, and ride north of the river in rush hour all the way to his house. When he told me the details later I was amazed. The right-hand footpeg was buckled to the point it was vertical and he'd also had to kick-start the BSA. The gear change is on the right-hand side of those old bikes and it was Ewan's right leg that was broken. Ironically, since that peg was vertical he was able to get his foot fully under the shifter and change gear without having to flex his ankle. Again, that lulled him into thinking there was no way he could've broken the leg.

He called me as soon as he got home and said he was going to Casualty. Of course, when he got there the leg was X-rayed and the break confirmed. I remember being pretty gobsmacked. The two of us had done numerous track days together and ridden all the way around the world without serious injury, and there he was taken down by a pedestrian on Holland Road.

After the boys left I took a good look at the Exogen machine. It's designed to assist bone growth, and when I checked the blurb it claimed to enhance even non-union breaks (established by Exogen as 'when the fracture site shows no visibly progressive signs of healing') to the tune of 86 per cent. I had to use it for 20 minutes every day; it works by sending ultrasound waves through the skin and soft tissue to the fracture, where cell receptors set off a 'cascade' of reactions and upregulate processes critical to bone repair. I was up for it, no matter the cost. I may not have had a Zimmer to help me get around, but I had ultrasound and a pair of crutches that didn't chafe my palms. The most important thing was that I was no longer tied to the wheelchair.

I'd been so pissed off by the chair, I cannot tell you. The only good thing that came of it was seeing Trevor Jones, an old friend who I'd hadn't seen for ages who'd been paralysed in a skiing accident. He heard I'd had the crash and got in touch, and I invited him over for dinner. Trevor used to be a Royal Navy helicopter pilot and was a really active sportsman. Now he's wheelchair-bound, and sadly it's permanent. He told me he was gutted I'd been hurt but it was good to have someone to talk to who was functioning at the same physical level as he was. He said it was great to be able to look someone in the face rather than up at them as he had to with able-bodied people.

He's an amazing man. Back in 1987 when he was flying rescue missions for the Royal Navy, he fished Richard Branson out of the Irish Sea after he and Per Lindstrand had almost completed their transatlantic crossing in a hot-air balloon. They had been making for the Mull of Kintyre when low clouds forced them to descend from 27,000 feet.

They hit the ground near a place called Limavady in Northern Ireland, lost two of their fuel tanks, and managed to get back in the air only to land on the water between Northern Ireland and Scotland. They fired the explosive bolts to release the balloon from the capsule but they did not work. After that they were dragged through the water by the wind; Branson says the speeds were up to 100mph with water flooding into the capsule, so both men climbed out. The balloon bounced airborne again and Lindstrand jumped into the sea without a life jacket. Branson was still with the balloon, and was considering jumping with a parachute – but the balloon went down again and he too leapt into the sea, by now miles from where Lindstrand had been.

He was a floating dot in the ocean when Trevor located him. It was pretty soon after he went in and he didn't suffer too badly, but Lindstrand spent two hours swimming before he was found and rescued as well.

Without Trevor those two guys wouldn't be around today, and tragically within a few years he would be in a wheelchair. He was skiing in a race in the Alps, competing on a course which had been cordoned off – yet as he made a turn he found himself speeding towards some spectators who had managed to get on the course. Swerving to avoid them, he veered around a marker on the very edge of the mountain. It was his only option, but he had no way of knowing that it had been uprooted earlier then put back in the wrong place – too close to the brink and the drop to a carpark below. Unable to stop, Trevor went over the edge.

It was a freak accident, but it changed his life forever. Just like me, he was doing something he loved, and I guess we were both unlucky. Of course, my life hasn't been changed to the extent Trevor's has – the way he's dealt with what happened to him has been truly amazing. I can still get around, albeit with difficulty, and I doubt I'll walk without a limp again, but I still count myself very lucky.

I should've seen more of Trevor. I should've seen more of lots of people, but I'd been so busy just trying to get well. Not long after I got my crutches I had another bout of appointments lined up with the orthopaedic and plastic surgeons. We still weren't at the point they'd marked as D-Day yet, and that was always on my mind. That said, it was no longer quite so ominous because now I was out of the wheelchair I was moving my left leg much more effectively, and I took that to be a good sign.

Another trip to the Lindo Wing; Olly wanted me to stay in the chair because the only place we'd been able to park the last time was some distance from the main entrance and she wasn't sure I could make it on crutches. I was having none of it. I never wanted to sit in that chair again. The Beckham boot was gone and my ankle was rotating nicely, and I was going to walk as best I could. It was a couple of hundred yards and that was the furthest I'd gone so far.

I made it alright, though I have to admit it was an effort. I got up the steps and headed for the lift and went up to the suite where the X-rays were taken and when that was over,

I crossed the road to the set of steps made famous by the Duchess of Cambridge when she appeared with new-born baby George. As usual, couples who'd had their babies delivered that day were taking selfies and during my time traipsing in and out I'd held the camera for quite a few.

Checking in at reception, I sat down to wait for the surgeons to come out of theatre. These guys are so busy, flitting from operation to consultation and back to operation again, I don't know how they keep track. Despite all that, the attention I received from both of them and the detail they went into was incredible. Dinesh (the orthopaedic surgeon) told me the X-rays looked alright, and what he could see in terms of activity around the fracture site was about what he'd expected − although the substantial piece of bone that was the focal point did appear to still be isolated. He said that didn't necessarily mean it was going to die, but we would just have to wait and see. Apart from that there was reasonable alignment and no bone displacement since the last set of X-rays, and that sounded positive enough. I wasn't sure really, he seemed to see progress but when I looked at the pictures it didn't look as though anything was happening at all.

He commented that the calf was soft and not swollen and tender − which was a good thing − and my foot was moving well. He was pleased to hear I was using the Exogen machine and told me to make sure I did those 20 minutes every day. He could see I was on crutches now, of course, and he was delighted about that. He's a pretty brusque sort of guy, and as I've hinted that can sometimes be a little daunting, but when it comes to the positives that kind of bluntness is what you want.

So I left that appointment thinking I was making progress, but there was still that date lying in wait in early June. I don't know why, but despite the surgeon's words I could not get away from the foreboding feeling that when D-Day arrived, the news would not be good.

On the way home I spoke to Ewan on the phone. I told him what was going on and he was delighted for me. He mentioned he'd been talking to a journalist from New York and once again the questions were all about the bike trips and whether he and I were finally going to do *Long Way Up*. It's the last voyage in our global journey of discovery. From the southern tip of South America to Alaska – we'll get to it one day, I'm sure of it.

Just as I hung up the phone a pedestrian stepped out from between a couple of parked cars and Olly had to stamp on the brakes. The guy lifted an apologetic hand and I looked on as he made the pavement, shaking my head.

'That's what we were most worried about when we rode through Africa,' I said. 'Remember, Olly – the pedestrians? We were terrified we'd run someone down and especially after what happened to Ewan.'

It was true. As we'd mapped the route and made plans for *Long Way Down*, our African expedition, we'd talked about the need to be ultra-careful. When we rode around the world we went through some serious country but most of the time it was remote and there weren't that many people around. In Africa it was different; the roads are the arteries of the continent and the majority of people don't have vehicles. Unlike the main road links in the west, people walk African tarmac all the time and one of our major worries had been the risk of hitting someone. As it turned out, that episode in London was the only time it happened and we encountered no such dramas in Africa.

There were a couple of incidents that stuck in my mind, however; with all the recent talk about 'limb salvation', one kept returning to me again and again. That was in Ethiopia and I'll come to it in a minute. By the time we got there, though, we'd covered a lot of miles having ridden across Europe to Sicily then taken a ferry to Tunisia. We'd ridden east from there and nearly been blown away by a sandstorm one night as we made our way to Leptis Magna.

Leptis Magna is an ancient Roman city dating back hundreds of years BC and, according to the guy who showed us around, it's known mainly as the city of Septimius Severus, a native who became Roman Emperor and died in York of all places.

In Rome we'd ridden the old Appian Way and now we were walking a road that led from the great Arch of Septimius Severus all the way to Alexandria. In the other direction, it stretched as far as Carthage. It was incredible; it had been smashed to pieces centuries before but in 1920 a group of Italian archaeologists had excavated the stones and reconstructed it. Some of the stones were decorated with images of Septimius and his sons – copies apparently, with the originals housed in a museum in Tripoli. There were these huge triangles that our guide told us were actually Venetian and from a much later period, but were there to keep evil spirits away. Eight pillars seemed to climb from the floor, topped by eight godlike figures with a crown in one hand and a palm in the other, as well as four eagles – the ancient symbol of power used by both the Nazis and the Americans. There was an image of the goddess Diana and another of Apollo and I commented to Ewan that he was hung like a donkey.

'Don't let him hear you say that,' Ewan said.

'He won't mind, it's a compliment – and he's a god, right? He's meant to be well endowed.'

We walked the streets, which were cambered and had been fed with running water drawn from wadis to supply the whole city.

'There would've been shops here,' I said. 'Businesses, lots of people milling about just like Rome.'

'Yeah, only not so many mopeds.' Ewan arched one eyebrow. In Rome, we'd not been able to move for almost being knocked off our bikes by mopeds.

'No, but they'd have chariots to tear about in,' I said. 'The kids I mean. You know, pulled by greyhounds or something.'

We came to another corner and another naked penis. There had been a few already in this city, only this one had wings. Our guide explained that the winged penis was the

defender of the city and it was doing battle with the evil eye.
He said it was another symbol used to keep evil spirits away
and had been there since the second century. He told us it
was good luck to touch it, so, with a brief exchange of
glances, Ewan and I pressed a hand to it for luck on the rest
of our way.

'Well, mate,' Ewan said in a matter-of-fact sort of tone.
'We've touched a penis in Libya. Not what we set out to do
perhaps, but it is at least a winged penis.'

'It was placed there in the time of communists,' our
guide stated.

'Communists?' Ewan said. 'In the second century?
Jesus, really, I don't know anything about anything. I thought
Communism was Marx and Lenin, Russia in the First
World War.'

'He said Commodus,' another voice piped up; Claudio,
our so-far silent cameraman. 'The Roman Emperor
Commodus, Ewan, not Communist.' We'd misunderstood
the guide completely – and it's a fact Claudio knew more
about the places we passed through on that journey than the
rest of the team put together.

From Libya, we crossed into Egypt and visited the pyramids.
We had an 'ice-cold beer in Alex' before riding all the way
to Lake Nasser and taking a boat into the Sudan. From there
it was Ethiopia and the horn of Africa where we made our
way across the stunning highland region to hook up with a
team from UNICEF in the ancient city of Axum. It's world

renowned for the vertical pillars of stone they call Stelae, but it's also where the Queen of Sheba's palace was unearthed. We didn't stay long enough to see the Stelae or the palace, however; after a brief stop for food and a shower we took an unbelievably rugged road towards the border with Eritrea.

'The road at the end of the world': that's what we called it and that's exactly what it looked like in the wake of the war between Ethiopia and Eritrea. UNICEF had asked us to highlight the plight of the countless children who'd had their lives altered forever by the indiscriminate use of landmines. They're a particular hate of both Ewan and I and when we arrived there were a million unmapped mines still buried along the border.

The two countries had been fighting on and off for years, but the most recent conflict was between 1998 and 2000. After that a shaky ceasefire had been brokered, and when we got there in 2007 a 25 kilometre-wide 'Temporary Security Zone' was still in place. It was patrolled by a rotation of UN troops, many of whom were based in Adigrat, a crazy town where the power supply was always being interrupted. While we were there the lights went out and I mean all the lights; it was so dark you couldn't see anything.

With the presence of those troops the ceasefire had held and a mine-clearing operation was underway that was painstakingly difficult and dangerous. It costs just $3 to lay a landmine but $1,000 to destroy it.

The first morning we were there we drove out towards the ruined town of Zalambessa, which had been massively under dispute during the war and now marked the edge of the Security Zone. The young man we wanted to see lived a hundred yards off the road in a village called Addis Tesfa. I'll never forget the place, constructed from mud and thatch among cacti and acacia on a high plateau; windswept, desolate. The young man's name was Tesfu and he was slightly built with a skinny little moustache tracing his upper lip. When he was young he'd been a keen footballer but he'd dropped out of school at the age of 14 and hadn't played football since.

Ethiopia is among the poorest countries in the world and 85 per cent of the population is illiterate. Despite that, people like Tesfu are acutely aware that education is critical if they want to have a future that isn't tied to the land in the kind of subsistence farming that's still locked in the Dark Ages. Ethiopians are an incredibly beautiful and friendly people who suffer great hardship every day, yet carry on with a smile. They tend to be outgoing and Tesfu was no different, although he was very softly spoken.

Eight years previously the war was raging with Eritrea so he and his family had to take refuge in Adigrat, where they remained for two years until the cautious peace was established. After that they went back to their village to find their home was no longer habitable, so that same afternoon they set about building a new one.

As they started work the whole family were trotting in and out of the old house without any problems, though unbeknown to any of them a mine had been laid right outside the door. When I think how callous that was my

256

blood boils. It was just a matter of time of course, and on the third day back from Adigrat Tesfu was up there on his own.

He remembers the time it happened exactly: four o'clock in the afternoon, he was 14 years old. He stepped on the mine – and that was the last thing he remembered until he woke up in hospital four days later, his right leg amputated. Fortunately there had been a soldier close by who heard the blast and got to Tesfu in time to save his life. When we met him he'd been without that leg for six years and the prosthetic he'd been given was so ancient the foot was broken. It was held together with duct tape.

PART FIVE

6 June – 6 September 2016:

London, England

D-DAY

Over the next few weeks I gradually began to get stronger. It was very slow progress and though I could bear a little more weight on my left foot, all of it was displaced by the frame. My right side felt a lot better, except for the fact I was favouring it. I could get around. I was itching to be more independent. As far as I was concerned, being back on two wheels in any form was another waypoint on my road to full recovery.

By now I was rid of the boot and was putting more than 50 per cent weight on my ankle, which was a major step forward. The big deal though was getting the moped on and off its centre stand. I didn't think taking it off would be too much of a problem, but I didn't want to try until I was sure I could get it back on again. I hobbled back inside the house and rang Roy to ask him if he had any side-stands that could be fitted to the moped. He'd dealt with mopeds when he had his shop, and told me he had one knocking about and he'd see if he could put his hands on it. I was itching to go now so I shuffled outside again and worked out that I could probably get the moped back on its stand by wedging the bottom of a crutch against the base.

Beginning to get excited now, I took off the waterproof cover from the foot well – and to do that I had to actually get down on my knee. I managed that, which was another first, then I rolled the moped off the stand. Carefully I sat on it with my left foot in the foot well and my right on the ground, and everything felt OK. Of course, I started the motor and before I could have any second thoughts I was on the road, not even remembering a helmet. I rode up the street, the first time I'd been on two wheels in six months. The sense of freedom, the exhilaration, was incredible.

I got to the end of the road and suddenly noticed my lack of a helmet; I thought I'd better turn around as I didn't want to attract the attention of any passing policeman. When I got back to the house I saw Doone in the drive holding her laptop, an incredulous expression on her face. I think she must've been watching a movie or something in the kitchen and came out when she heard the sound of the engine starting.

'Dad,' she said. 'What the fuck are you doing?'

I know, it's something we need to address; the language in our house is terrible.

'Oh,' I said, 'I'm just making sure the bike works for Olly.'

'What?' she said. 'What the fuck does that mean?' She told me to get the moped back in the drive and come inside. 'It's not good,' she said. 'You can barely hobble. What if you fall over? You could really do some damage then.'

I had no intention of getting off the bike. I knew she was going out, so with a cheeky grin I said, 'If you grab the helmets I'll give you a lift over Hammersmith Bridge.'

She didn't need telling twice. Moments later I had a helmet on and my daughter was on the back of the moped as we headed towards the bridge. I dropped her off and then rode back again and managed to get the bike on its centre stand using the base of my crutch.

Finally, it was upon me. The day I'd been dreading; I had it noted in the diary on my phone. I hobbled out to the car as Olly loaded Ziggy into the back; he hates to be left behind. I was quiet, pensive, the silence taking over again as we drove across London to Paddington. We had to leave the dog in the car, but it was shady and cool and I hobbled along the pavement to the entrance where the hardened smokers were gathered with their incongruous mix of intravenous drips, pyjamas and fags.

I could smell the scent of coffee drifting from the shop on the left as I made my way to the lift. Up to the third floor I hobbled along the corridor to X-ray where the same woman I always saw was at the desk.

'Mr Boorman,' she said, looking up in surprise. 'We weren't expecting you. Is something wrong?'

'No,' I said. 'Nothing's wrong. I'm here for an X-ray. I've got a consultation with Mr Simmons and Mr Nathwani.'

'Are you sure?' She was scouring the computer screen in front of her.

'Positive,' I said. 'It's the big meeting, the consultation where they tell me if I'm going to need another operation.'

'I can't find you,' she said. 'I'm sorry. You're not booked in for an X-ray this morning.'

'Sure I am.' I was beginning to panic. This was all I needed after months and months of trepidation. I checked my phone. 'June 6th,' I said. 'My appointment is June 6th. It's here in my...'

Only it wasn't, I realised as she shook her head, pointing at the computer screen. June 6th wasn't listed; the appointment was for June 7th.

So that was it. I had to hobble to the lift and go back down to the ground floor, across the concourse into the busy street and all the way back to the car. We traipsed home again with nothing resolved because I'd got the date mixed up.

I could not believe I'd been such an idiot. How could I have got the date wrong? I mean, this was the most important day of my recovery and I'd put the wrong date in my diary. All the way across London we drove in silence. I was absolutely gutted. When we finally arrived back at the house I went to work on the Exogen machine to keep my mind from running away with itself. When that was done I concentrated on some of the exercises my physiotherapist had given me. Initially they were fairly lightweight, just designed to get the muscles working and blood flowing properly. As time went on I was hoping they would extend to a fixed bicycle and this sort of half-length 'surfboard' that pivoted on a large rubber ball. That was all on my right leg – the physiotherapy had no bearing on the piece of bone they'd pinned after it seemed to be floating free. I still didn't know if it was where the surgeons wanted it to be or not and my whole future was riding on it. If the news wasn't good I'd need a bone graft, and I'd been sweating on that for so long already, yet now I had to sweat for another day.

After another semi-sleepless night, I woke to an ache in my stomach that felt like a physical pain. A gnawing sensation, a sickness, nausea that lifted as bile in my throat. I was in a really bad mood, really quiet; I'd sunk into silence and was exuding this sense of doom and gloom that filtered through to my wife.

She had to be as frustrated with the last few months as I was. When we arrived at the Lindo Wing she stopped in the middle of the road to get the pay-to-park number rather than pull into the space. We were likely to block the traffic while she tried to pay so I told her to just park the car and pay then. She ignored me completely. Totally nonplussed, she went on trying to pay on her phone and gradually the cars backed up behind us. People started honking their horns and I told her to just park the fucking car. We had a serious row before she finally put her phone down and backed into a parking space.

That's how I remember it anyway. I'm sure Olly would say it wasn't like that at all. Whichever way it was, it was fraught and tempestuous, but with the car out of the road I got down and stood resting my weight on the crutches. This was it, 7 June 2016. Finally, I'd know if I was on the road to recovery or right back where I started.

Making my way up the road I tried to put a brave face on it, telling myself that I'd deal with the outcome no matter what it was. We were a little early for the X-ray at 12.30 and Olly wanted a sandwich. Food was the last thing on my mind, but we got the sandwich and she ate it outside at a table while I sat and stared at the doors to the Lindo Wing.

Fifteen minutes later I was on the third floor of the main hospital having the X-rays taken that I'd thought I'd have yesterday. Ten minutes after that it was back in the lift then across the road where I had to wait for Dinesh and Jon.

When they finally came in, they called up the X-ray on the computer screen and as far as I could tell the piece of bone looked as isolated as it always had. There was quiet in the room as both surgeons inspected the pictures, and I closed my eyes as I waited to hear the worst.

'Actually, it's looking pretty good.' I think it was Dinesh who spoke, the orthopaedic surgeon, but it might've been Jon. 'There are signs of fusion between those two extremities now and the bone is very much alive. Charley,' he said. 'You'll be pleased to know we're about where we thought we would be.'

I could not believe my ears. 'So it's working?' I was looking at Olivia; I was almost crying. 'I won't need the bone graft now?'

'No,' Dinesh shook his head. 'You're making real progress; we're where we hoped we would be.'

I still did not quite believe him because the wire that held that crucial piece of bone was bothering me and I thought that must be a bad sign. But then it had been like that pretty much since they'd put it in, always feeling as if it wasn't quite in the right place and maybe that's just the way it had to be. But as I sat stretched out on the bed I could feel it pushing against my calf. They took a good look, especially plastic surgeon Jon, examining the pin sites in my leg. He said they were maybe a little inflamed but it was nothing to be concerned about.

Then Dinesh told me it was time to bear some weight on the cage. He asked me to stand up and I was so shocked I just stared at him. I'd had the frame on since the beginning of March and so far that hadn't even been an option.

'Go on,' the surgeon said, 'it's time. See if you can put some weight on it.'

Still I looked at Olly. I wasn't sure I could stand and neither was she. I could see the horror in her eyes as if she thought I would just collapse.

I couldn't manage it by myself so Jon stood one side and Dinesh the other, and they supported my arms as I swung my battered legs off the bed.

Both feet on the floor. 7 June 2016. For the first time in months I walked.

It was amazing, I cannot describe the feeling of relief. Just moments before I'd been looking at those X-rays thinking that nothing had changed and here I was – walking.

My joy was pretty short-lived. Just two weeks later I was back in that same consulting room, having woken up with a lot of pain in my leg. I was sweating, panicking; I got on the phone to the hospital and the surgeons agreed to see me right away. I hobbled in, still weight-bearing, but telling them the pin sites were giving me serious gyp. They examined the leg and the plastic surgeon told me that the pain was probably just due to the fact that I was putting some weight on my left foot. When he looked at the pins he said they were actually in better shape than when he saw me two weeks ago. He admitted that my leg was a bit more swollen, but again, that was due to the fact I was more upright and mobile. Apparently the extension in my knee had improved and there was no tenderness when he palpated my calf. He assured me that all was well and I had nothing to worry about; that I should go home and continue with the physiotherapy.

I knew that was really important, and it wasn't just Pippa at Rosslyn Park I'd be working with – as soon as I was better I planned to go and see Dreas. He's a guy my dad found to help me with posture when I was a teenager. Part of my psychological withdrawal as a child had some physical manifestations that came much later. I say physical – they were, but the cause was not muscular or anything bone-related. I developed a hunch as some kind of inadvertent self-protection mechanism. I think I was so infused with this sense of inadequacy that I was tense all the time, so much so that the muscles in my back and shoulders seized and I began to stoop. I'm not the tallest guy in the world so it was noticeable pretty quickly. I carried that stance until Dreas got to work on me. He's an ex-ballet dancer and to this day specialises in body conditioning using an aggressive form of Pilates. He created a series of exercises for me that not only addressed the physical manifestation but the mental state that created them in the first place. He taught me to relax my mind and relax the muscles in a way that actually strengthened them. By the time we were done I didn't only stand straight, I added an inch in height.

I saw Dreas again only recently and I'm planning to do some more work with him when my leg is fully recovered. He's 80 now but looks more buff and muscular than many guys I know in their 30s.

Despite that scary morning of pain I was making progress; things were going well and when I saw the surgeons again on 19 July they took out that irritating pin. It had been causing me more trouble and a lot more pain and I didn't feel as if it was doing any good. When they checked the X-rays they decided that it didn't need to be there anymore, so the orthopaedic surgeon went off to fetch a pair of pliers from B&Q. No, I'm joking – that's where he said he was going; he didn't have the right tools to hand so he hunted down a pair of stainless steel forceps. When he came back he went to work on my leg, telling me it wouldn't hurt.

It was agony – I mean really painful; the surgeon with the pliers and me holding the leg, another tug of war like the dance I'd performed with Rupert Eckersley. There was no 'manning up' to be done here though – the plastic surgeon thought there was a tiny barb on the wire and that's what was catching. It was so painful they gave me a shot of local anaesthetic, but didn't wait long enough for it to kick in. Dinesh got right into it and after another substantial tug of war, the length of wire popped out of the skin.

Eventually, when I'd stopped sweating, I asked them when they thought I might be able to have the frame taken off. Dinesh took another look at the X-rays.

'Well,' he said. 'The bone is fusing but to help things along we could always knock a nail in.'

He was talking to his colleague rather than me, but those were the words he used as he sat looking at the screen.

'Hang on a minute,' Olly said. 'Knock a nail in – what do you mean?'

Glancing at her the surgeon indicated the screen. 'See where there's still a gap around that piece of bone?' He indicated the section of bone that the wire had been holding just now. 'It still needs support and the frame might be enough, but it might not. If we drop a nail in, that would give it a little more strength.'

'But doesn't that increase the risk of infection?' Olly said.

Dinesh nodded. 'It does.'

'So why do it?'

'If you want the frame off quicker it's a suggestion.' He glanced at Jon. 'What do you think?'

Before the plastic surgeon could get involved, I did. 'If you do that,' I said, 'will I be more mobile?'

'Much,' Dinesh informed me. 'You'll have support in the leg. Your right ankle is pretty well fixed now; you'll be walking around quite quickly.'

'How quickly? I'm supposed to be on a motorbike tour in South America in September – could I make that?'

'You might,' he conceded. 'But not on a motorbike.'

'What about in a car?'

'I wouldn't recommend it, but it's possible.'

I looked at Olly, who was shaking her head. The surgeon took another look at the X-ray. 'But your wife is right,' he said. 'It raises the risk of infection. If anything should go wrong and you're in the middle of nowhere…I think for now we'll leave the frame where it is.'

A PROPER CHARLEY

I left the hospital and headed back to the car feeling really hopeful, though Olly was against the idea of any kind of new metal in my leg even if it would speed up the recovery. Having come this far, she argued, why risk the threat of infection? The whole point of the frame had been to remove that risk and allow the bone to knit properly.

There was no arguing with that and my only issue was the fact I was going to miss another motorbike tour. I spoke to Billy and he said he'd let the clients know. Up until then we'd been keeping them informed of my progress on social media. We had a back-up plan that involved Claudio taking my place with the added bonus that he'd film some of the trip, which was a first for any of our guests.

I was gutted though; I hate letting anyone down and this was the very first expedition to a part of the world I've never been to. If I could make the second tour at the end of the month, it would be great – but what the surgeon had said about anything going wrong abroad bothered me, and Olly pointed out that the insurance company wouldn't facilitate a medivac a second time. It had cost £18,000 for the air ambulance from Portugal so God knows what it would cost to fly me home from Chile.

I couldn't risk it. I'd come this far, but even so I told myself that I still might make that second trip at the end of September. Dropping Olly off at home, I headed south of London to my lock-up. The state of the chrome on my bobber's forks had been in the back of my mind, and I wanted to check it out. The lock-up is on a friend's farm and it's great because it's free, but it is a little damp. It's where Roy and I built my Kawasaki W650 rat bike, and there's another build underway that's been on the back burner since I had the accident.

The bobber isn't the only bike I keep there. I've got a mad sportsbike that BMW gave me while I was working with them. The HP2 Sport is a gorgeous limited build they put together before they brought out the S1000RR, where the engineers did some wacky stuff with the boxer engine. There's carbon fibre everywhere, a quickshifter and a superbike dash display that shows the revs and lap times rather than the speed you're going, though you can switch it to a speedo for use on the road. It's pretty much a full-on track bike and a collector's item; I was lucky they agreed to let me have it.

My Dakar race bike is in the lock-up too and I stroke it lovingly whenever I'm down there. We had four made but mine was the first so we could mess around, trying all the Touratech add-ons and making the mistakes to ensure the others were built to an exact specification.

As soon as I opened the door I could see just how bad the rust on the bobber was. It was much worse than when I had seen it the last time. It wasn't just rusting, it was bubbling, peeling off, and I had to do something about it. I didn't ride the bike as much as I'd like even before my accident, and I would address that situation as well as the chrome just as soon as I was able.

I'd got the idea from Ewan after we finished making *Long Way Down*. The Baron's Speed Shop had built a bike for him that was absolutely stunning. I fancied having one put together as well so I could ride it at the beginning of the *By Any Means* expedition I made with Russ Malkin and Paul 'Mungo' Mungeam, who is Bear Grylls' lead cameraman now. That was when we travelled from my childhood home in County Wicklow to Sydney, by any means we could find to make the journey. The first stage was on a motorbike of course; I'd wanted something different and a custom-made bobber was perfect. I spoke to Dick and Del who own the Speed Shop about what kind of bike I wanted. They only make individual machines and they're made to order. I had some firm ideas so the three of us sat down and they sketched out the kind of thing I was describing. I wanted something short in the frame, a little squashed I suppose, with fabric wrapped around the exhaust to make it more of a rat bike. They took the ideas and those sketches and a few days later I got a call from Del. 'Look Charley,' he said. 'About this bike, mate. I've had an epiphany.'

Pretty excited about how enthusiastic he sounded, I jumped on my bike and rode across town to their workshop in Croydon. Both Dick and Del were there and Del repeated that he had indeed had what he called an epiphany.

'Charley,' he said, leading me over to the workbench. 'I know what you told us but I think this is the bike we should build.' He showed me the sketches he had made and it was nothing like the bike I'd described at all. The more I looked at the pictures the more I could see it was exactly the kind of bike they liked to build and, to be fair, they're very good at it. I didn't mind. The design was amazing and, looking back now, I get the feeling they humoured me for as long as they thought they needed to, then produced a sketch of the bike they intended to build from the get-go.

I told them to go for it and they just about managed to get it done in time for the beginning of the journey. Triumph-based, a twin of course; the motor was recovered and reconditioned from an engine brought out in 1959. The frame was styled and built from scratch with a racing crank to give it a bit of va-va-voom. It's a hardtail so it's not that comfortable; no rear suspension and both front and back brakes are old fashioned drums. They're not very effective, especially when compared to modern bikes, but they have to be in keeping with the theme of the bike as a whole. The gear shifter is on the right rather than the left, so I had to get used to that. But it looks awesome, with a cherry-red petrol tank and high lift bars. The state of the forks was really pissing me off now. I'd have to get the bike out of here and have it re-chromed. It shouldn't be there anyway; it should be on display in my living room. Maybe I'll figure out a way I can do that – I'll have to talk to my wife.

Everything was going so well. July crept into August, and on the 23rd my twin sister Daisy and I celebrated our 50th birthday with 40 of our closest friends. That weekend was the bank holiday and Olly had arranged to play tennis with Daisy and our great friend Paula. I'd been chatting to my mate Dom who lives down the road and he suggested breakfast in the Bike Shed.

I needed something to cheer me up because by that time we'd decided there was no way I'd make the second trip to South America, never mind the first. When that realisation hit me it brought tears to my eyes because I knew every single guest who'd be riding. They'd all been on at least one other tour with me and some of them two or three. I was absolutely gutted. I was moving around much better than I had been and I was doing physio on the bike and 'surfboard'. I was making massive strides, only they weren't massive enough to get me on a plane to South America.

Anyway, Dom texted to suggest breakfast for a bunch of us for around 10.30. Originally I wasn't going to go – and now I wish I hadn't. I sent him a text that said 'Sorry, I've run out of time'.

Why I said that I have no idea, and he immediately sent me another text. 'What the fuck are you talking about? Out of what fucking time?'

I really didn't know what I meant; maybe I'd had some kind of premonition. By now Daisy and Paula had arrived and they were in the kitchen with Olly, drinking tea and making a racket, so I wouldn't be missed. I sent Dom another text telling him I'd go.

At ten minutes to ten I was outside leaning on my stick. I still had the crutches, but most of the time I was using a stick now. I had a bit of an inspection of the moped, remembering that the waterproof cover was a little loose, so I set about tightening it up. Twisting the handlebars to full lock I fiddled around and got it sorted, only I didn't see that part of the cover had caught between the bars and the faring. I got on the bike and started the engine, then went to accelerate at the same time as straightening the handlebars. I was literally right outside the front door, but due to that caught cover the handlebars didn't straighten and the moped went down on its side with a bang.

I didn't see it coming, and I smacked my hip so hard on the ground I almost passed out. For a second I just lay there still encased by the waterproof cover, not sure if I'd bashed the frame around my leg or not. I couldn't feel anything except this terrible pain in my hip. Fortunately a girl was passing by the house and she saw the bike fall over. She was the first to get to me; she helped get it off me and then she rang the doorbell. Olly answered and when she saw me she literally howled.

At the same moment Dom turned up on his bike to see what was going on because by now I was late. He helped me up while Olly went inside for a stool. She set it down just as I got free of the waterproof cover. With Dom's help I managed to sit on the stool, trying to get my head around what just happened. The pain in my hip was excruciating and I really began to worry.

'Jesus,' I said, trying to catch my breath. 'I've fucked this up. I've really fucked this up. I think I've broken my hip.'

Stripping away the protective cover I keep around the frame I could see blood at each of the pin sites. Now the worry turned to panic. Blood on my leg and a busted hip – I told Olly I had to go to the hospital. She phoned for an ambulance right away and they showed up pretty quickly. They looked me over carefully before lifting me onto yet another gurney. I couldn't believe it, lights and sirens again; and before I knew it, I was back at the Chelsea and Westminster. The paramedics wheeled me in and as they handed me over to the nurses they said something that deepened my sense of depression even further. It might not sound like much, but right then it was everything to me.

'Possible hip break,' they said. 'Boorman – Charley – male – 50.'

Fifty years old, and I was lying on that fucking gurney staring at fluorescent lights as if I was some old wreck of a man. Certain I'd set my recovery back after all we'd gone through, I just wanted to curl up and die. They took me into X-ray and the doctor called up the history so he could make a comparison with how the leg looked now and how it had been.

'Wow,' he said when he saw the extent of the fracture. 'You were lucky not to lose that leg.'

'Yeah I know,' I said. 'What does it look like? Have I done any more damage? Have I dislodged any pins?'

For a moment, he didn't answer. Then he pushed out his lips and narrowed his eyes – and finally, he shook his head. 'No,' he said, 'it doesn't look like it to me.'

I wasn't sure I believed him, but at least it turned out that there was no fracture in my hip. They let me out and I came home totally incapacitated. Just that morning I'd been walking with a stick and earlier in the week I'd hosted my birthday party. The only time I'd used crutches was when I was really knackered, just before I went to bed. Now I was in so much pain I couldn't move. I'd been sleeping upstairs for well over a month and now I was right back on the sofa.

As the week wore on and the pain in my hip didn't get any better, I grew more and more convinced I'd really fucked up. I could barely get off the sofa and my mood was as bad as it had ever been. Anyone I spoke to was given short shrift, and even the dog avoided me. It was my own stupid fault, and now not only was the South American tour beyond me, I was beginning to worry about the date for the Darien Gap.

My next appointment had been set for Tuesday 6 September and it took ages to get through the week. By the time the weekend came around I was back on the crutches, but there was no chance of using the stick. The only way I could get in and out of the car now was by using a small set of decorator's steps – just three rungs, the kind of thing you stand on to paint the top of a wall. I had to carry it out to the car and set it up, then hoist it after me with the handle of my crutch.

When Tuesday came around I went to the hospital with my daughter Doone. Olly was in Morocco on a ten-day break she had been really looking forward to, but when I fell off the moped she almost didn't go. I had to cajole her, persuade her, tell her that Tini (an old friend from school who was going with her) would be really disappointed if she didn't. I reminded her that she'd been looking after me for so long without a break she really had to go.

So it was Doone that showed up with me at the Lindo Wing and once the X-rays were done, we were joined by Russ, who was going to film the consultation for the TV show on the Darien Gap. I explained what an idiot I'd been trying to ride the moped that Sunday and how the fall had set me back to the point at which I was terrified all over again.

When I was done, Russ had some news of his own. For quite a while now we'd been trying to find a co-presenter for the show and finally come to an agreement with Steve-O from Jackass. For those of you who haven't come across him before, he was born in London to a Canadian mother and American father, and describes himself as clown, stuntman and rapper. In 2015 he was sentenced to 30 days in the LA county jail for climbing a crane at Hollywood's SeaWorld carrying an inflatable orca that bore the words 'SeaWorld Sucks'. When he got to the top of the crane he started setting off fireworks and was subsequently arrested.

Anyway, Steve-O was in the frame, but Russ told me that he'd had an accident whilst performing a stunt for

YouTube. He was on a skateboard on top of a wooden box, a 'porta-potty' thing, as a car drove into it. His plan had been to flip off the top, land flawlessly on the board and skate off looking super cool. Only that didn't happen. Instead he landed awkwardly and broke his right ankle in three places as well as his left heel. So, that was both of us out of the game, but even knowing I wasn't the only sucker for punishment didn't make me feel any better.

I have to admit that when the time came for the consultation I only told Dinesh I'd had a fall and not actually how it happened. I was really worried that the frame had shifted, and would probably have owned up if it had. But he examined me thoroughly and told me I had set myself back about three weeks in terms of recovery, but only in my level of movement. I was still suffering from a really bad pain in the groin area of my hip and he gave it a proper look over. All the time I was checking the X-rays on the computer screen but I couldn't tell if I'd done any more damage to my leg or not.

The surgeon told me the pain in my hip and groin was muscular, stretched tendons probably, and would get better with time. He assured me I hadn't done any permanent damage to my lower leg and the pin sites hadn't been compromised. I asked him if he was sure and he checked my leg again and again. He made me straighten and bend it, he had me lifting it off the bed, and then he checked the X-rays a second time. He told me there was nothing wrong and the bone had knit properly both above and below the piece that had caused all the worry. I could see a line of white in the X-ray where that too was beginning to fuse properly now.

'Charley,' he said. 'You're fine. If you hadn't had the fall, we might be sitting here talking about taking the frame off.'

'You're kidding me,' I said.

'No, I think with another month that bone will have fused to the point we could to that, though we still might drop that nail in.'

My heart rose and sank and rose and sank again. I tried to get my head around what he was he telling me. I could finally get rid of this frame – but even now they might put a nail in?

'Why would we do that?' I said.

'To strengthen the leg. As I mentioned the last time you were here it will increase your ability to get around. Putting pressure on the bone stimulates growth and the more you're able to get around the more pressure you're going to create.'

'But what about infection?' It was Doone instead of Olly to pipe up with the objection this time.

'It's a risk,' Dinesh said. 'But a manageable one. If we decide the bone needs that extra strength, then we won't perform both operations at the same time. We'll get the frame off first and see how your dad gets on. If we need to drop a nail in, we'll do that as a separate procedure after.'

There was silence in the room while I digested the implications of what the surgeon had told me. 'So the next time you see me,' I said. 'If you're happy with what that piece of bone is doing you might book me in to take the frame off.'

'That's the idea,' Dinesh said.

I was ecstatic; right then I didn't care what the implications would be. I didn't care about a nail in my leg and I was sure I'd be past the point of infection. My natural optimism told me that as long as I didn't do anything stupid now this frame was coming off and I'd be mobile again.

Russ was getting it all on film and I was thinking how the footage would make a great 'sizzle' piece, so I asked the surgeon when he thought I'd be fit enough to take on the jungle and swamps of the Darien Gap. I needed that to be no later than March of 2017 or there was a good chance Channel 5 would bail.

Dinesh looked at me for a long moment and then he looked at Russ.

'No time soon,' he said. 'It'll be a year from now at least.'

PART SIX

7 September 2016 – 7 January 2017:

London, England

NON-UNION

Over the next few weeks I had to absorb the implications of that comment and what it would actually mean. With Channel 5 still backing us, I'd been counting on a Darien expedition in February 2017. That clearly wasn't going to happen, and a year from now the Gap would be impassable because of the rains. That meant the earliest opportunity we might have would be February 2018, two years from the original date we'd set. Two years of my working life lost the day I hit that wall. I couldn't quite believe it; this was the longest period I'd had on the sidelines, and it was beginning to weigh me down. But there were no guarantees that I'd make it even in 2018. So much could happen; the frame wasn't even off yet, and when I saw Dinesh again in early October he told me it would be yet another six weeks.

The scan was clear: although that one vital piece of bone was beginning to respond in the way the doctors had hoped, there was still no significant union with the lower half of my leg. Dinesh spoke again about inserting an 'intramedullary nail', and I began to wonder what the frame had been all about. Eight months of pain and awkwardness, interfering with everything from movement to sleep – and for what?

After all, it had been designed to replace the pin the Portuguese put in, which seemed to be what we were heading back to anyway. Something came back to me; something I'd heard from the doctor at A&E when I'd fallen off Olly's moped. He'd muttered something about the frame and the fact I was a celebrity, and that was the only reason it had been suggested in the first place. I hadn't taken any notice at the time, but it was bugging me now. I knew it shouldn't. My surgeon was no-nonsense, and the fact I was in showbiz made no difference to him. On the contrary, when we tried to film one of the consultations he reminded me that his job was to repair my leg and he refused to let 'my world' get in the way.

I ploughed on as best I could, trying to push all implications for the future to the back of my mind. I still had obligations to Triumph to take care of – there was another bike launch coming up, this time in London. They were about to reveal a brand new model to their range: the Bonneville Bobber, a classy-looking modern take on the retro style of the 1950s and 1960s with a single seat and set of drag-style bars.

The bike was revealed at a glitzy event at Printworks – as the name implies, an old printing works in east London. Triumph really pushed the boat out with a band playing, and a dragstrip set up at one end. Journalists from all over Europe were there as well as the great and good from the world of motorcycle racing. I showed up in my role as ambassador with Billy Ward and had the run of the place. It was packed; very little about the new bike had been published, and there was a sense of real expectation among the journalists. When the time came for the big reveal, four-time World Superbike Champion Carl Fogarty rode it onto the stage. The press corps gathered around taking pictures and trying to get the lowdown on the spec, although Triumph weren't releasing much – the only real information they had offered was the fact it was powered by the same 1200cc liquid-cooled motor they use on the Bonneville T120.

That's a lot of power for a bobber – usually they're 650cc or 750cc – and it was well demonstrated in a series of drag races that ran the length of the warehouse. Foggy took part as did 'Fast Freddie' Spencer. (You may remember him as the only racer to win both the 250cc and 500cc Grand Prix World Championship titles in the same year, 1985; a feat that will never be repeated with the demise of the 250 class.) Foggy lost his heat, and Foggy does not like losing. He's a winner, a true champion; it takes a certain kind of person to become a champion, and any loss is felt much more deeply than it would be by anyone else. Even though this was little more than a bit of fun, I could see how pissed off he was – he made no attempt to hide it. He never does. You could see by the look on his face he was as gutted as if he'd lost a world superbike race. The top guys are all like that, although some hide their disappointment better than others. Valentino Rossi, for instance, puts on a smile for the cameras, but I imagine inside he's seething.

Foggy wasn't the only British ex-racer there. Wandering around I saw Jamie Whitham, former British Superbike

Champion, and Steve Parrish, who was teammate to Barry Sheene with Suzuki back in the 1970s. There were loads of other people I knew from my trips to various paddocks, though as I chatted to them I sensed a hint of negativity.

I'd expected as much. It's always the same when a rider is injured; almost as if the bad luck that befell me that day in February might be contagious. Just a couple of weeks before that launch, I'd gone to Brands Hatch for the last round of the British Superbike Championship and bumped into Chris Walker. He took one look at my leg and shook his head.

'Sorry,' he said. 'I can't talk to you, Charley. Not today.' Quickly he bustled away.

It's nothing personal; that's just the way it is. No one wants to be around an injured biker in a racing paddock. The kind of thing that had happened to me can happen to any biker, racer or otherwise, and it's a hard thing to be reminded of; especially when you have to go out with a clear mind and push yourself. I understand that and, if I was in their shoes, I'd probably feel the same way.

So a few of the racers avoided me, but everyone else wanted to know what I'd done to my leg. I told the story so many times that night I got sick of the sound of my voice. In the end I started telling people that my wife had smashed my leg with a golf club. The expression on their faces said it all – not quite sure whether to believe me or not. It was a conversation killer, prompting a sort of strangled look and a few rushed words like 'OK, really, well, it's been very nice to see you...' And off they went. Sorry guys, I didn't mean to be rude – it's just that I'd been explaining what happened for months.

As the drag races continued I bumped into my old friend Adam Childs from *Motorcycle News*. Adam's a senior road tester, brilliant on a bike, and a couple of years ago he competed in the Isle of Man TT. He was racing the Junior class and I was lucky enough to be one of his 'pit bitches' (his words, not mine) – my job was to clean his helmet visor when he came in for a pit stop. I can't begin to explain how exciting it actually was. It gave me just a hint of what it must be like to be part of the crew in any kind of racing, be it bike or car. The rush is just incredible. At the TT, the riders don't come in until the end of the second lap, and since the circuit is 37.4 miles long there's a lot of time to hang around. You wait, and wait, and wait. Then suddenly it's time; they're in and the place is alive and you're part of it, even if your job is just to clean the rider's screen and visor. It's all part of making the stop as quick and efficient as possible. I had to make sure Adam's visor was clear otherwise he wouldn't be able to see where he was going clearly and that would affect his lap time.

I remember the sense of anticipation as the alarm sounded to tell us a pit stop was imminent. We knew roughly when it would be, of course, because we knew what time Adam was running and where he was on the track. The leader board at the Isle of Man is still maintained by hand, with numbers, times and race positions all sent back to the pit wall where local Cub Scouts keep the board updated.

The flow of adrenalin among the crew is almost as tangible as when you're actually riding. You wait and wait then a few riders start coming in and you're on tenterhooks, determined not to fuck up. As Adam crossed the line into pit lane he had to reduce his speed to the limit allowed and I watched keenly from our station. He got closer and closer; then it was all go, cloth in one hand and cleaning spray in the other.

There's a great video on YouTube that tells the story from the camera mounted on the frame of Adam's bike. Excellent footage of the racing – then the pit lane, where all you see is my crotch and the front wheel between my legs as I'm working away at the visor. Tank full and visor clear he was off again, leaving the pit crew so pumped we were high-fiving and chest-bumping – the rush was absolutely phenomenal.

Adam and I reminisced about that day in the paddock at the Bonneville Bobber launch, and then it was time for another drag race. I was standing right behind the bikes with a great view of the spinning rear wheels and smoke from belching exhausts. As the pair took off, I felt this massive bang right in the frame on my leg. It was like a gunshot, a sound that lifted above that of revving motorbikes – I thought I'd been hit by a piece of metal and instantly worried I'd further damaged the leg. The warehouse wasn't well lit, and when I looked down I couldn't see anything. I felt a bit of relief of pressure in the leg itself though. Ever since the frame was put on it's been under constant strain from the bolts and pins, but right at that moment it seemed to ease and I couldn't imagine why. I looked again but still couldn't see anything – until I noticed one of the wires had snapped where it had been bolted onto the frame. You can see from the photos how the wires go through the leg and attach on each side, and it was one of these that had gone. I was really freaked out. I could physically feel the blood draining from my face, sure my leg was about to fall apart. Leaning heavily on my walking stick and walking very gingerly with as much weight on my right leg as possible, I found Billy and told him what had happened and that we had to go.

We made our excuses and went back to the car. Back home I told Olly what had happened, and she looked closely at the frame and the loose wire and told me the other two seemed stable enough – there was nothing we could do until the morning. Perhaps I'd learned my lesson about putting off phone calls – first thing in the morning I phoned the orthopaedic surgeon, Dinesh. He told me not to worry; that wires snapping was sometimes a good sign because it showed strength in the bone, which is what we were trying to achieve. Luckily he was working at Charing Cross that morning and told me to come in at 12pm.

I duly arrived and headed to the examination room, where Dinesh said he would take the wire out. That brought on a bit of a sweat – I could still recall the last time he'd done it when the anaesthetic hadn't had time to kick in. He had a porter with him this time, though, who administered gas and air. He told me to suck on it before Dinesh started fiddling away with the wire so I'd be prepared. There's a teardrop on the wire which gives it the required traction on the bone, so the wire has to be pulled out exactly the right way or that teardrop will cause a rip. Dinesh seemed to be taking a while to figure out which way the wire was sitting; brow furrowed, sucking his teeth a little, he told me he was pretty sure he'd got it but couldn't be completely certain.

With the combination of gas and air it took a moment for me to realise he was joking. I remembered how brutal he'd been in his assessment when he first met me, and realised that after so many consultations I was not only getting to know him but also liked him a lot. He had the wire the right way of course, and while I sucked more gas and air he selected a pair of pliers from a ramshackle-looking toolbox. It was so old and beaten-up it looked as though it had been borrowed time and time again, the aged tools used and dumped back in the box with no order. I'm sure all was standard, the tools they used, but those pliers…in the state I was in, they looked wholly inappropriate for the job in hand.

He got the wire out with no real difficulty, and that left two to accompany me back – which very quickly became one. A few days after that first one snapped I was walking around at home and another went with no warning whatsoever – just ping! – and immediately I was on the phone.

Another consultation, more gas and air, and that same set of pliers…I was really pissed off now. I don't know why the mood hit so hard, but it's been like that at times since the accident and it seemed the whole thing was getting on top of me. Breaking wires, X-rays, CT scans that showed the kind of bone growth that didn't seem to be very good. Each time I saw him Dinesh talked about how we still might have to 'knock that nail in', and I couldn't help wondering what might've happened if they'd just left the plate that had been inserted when I was in Portugal.

I'd literally been home from the second wire removal for a just an hour or so when the last one snapped. I couldn't believe it; two in one day, three in a week, and now the whole top part of the frame was loose. I phoned the hospital again and spoke to Dinesh, who told me he couldn't do anything until the following Wednesday. At first I thought I could live with that. But with no wires at all to secure the top, the frame was flopping around and causing a lot of pain. With Wednesday still almost a week away I soon realised I couldn't wait that long and I phoned Dinesh back. After checking his diary, he suggested an operation to take the frame off first thing that coming Friday.

I couldn't quite believe that the frame would finally be off. In one sense the anticipation was great, but we weren't sure what it would mean. Right then I didn't care; I couldn't wait to be free of the thing and was keen to see what would happen next.

Any real hope I'd had was dashed pretty quickly when I came round from the operation. The frame was gone, which was a fantastic feeling, but I could tell by Dinesh's expression that all was not well. He told me he'd palpated the fracture site and there was still movement both left to right, and up and down. That indicated what he called 'delayed union', meaning the pieces of bone in my shin had not yet knit.

He said that we really had no choice now but to insert the nail and he would write as much to my GP. In the meantime I would have to wear another Beckham boot and bear as much weight on my leg as the pain would allow, while being back on the crutches again. That relief that I'd felt on finally waking up frame-free was crashing fast; I'd got to the point of walking almost unaided, but now I wouldn't be able to do anything again without a pair of crutches.

Dinesh explained that he would make an incision under my knee and move the kneecap to one side. Then he would slot in a hollow titanium nail running the length of my shin, securing it with bolts both at the knee and above my ankle. He explained that in order for the bone to fuse and regrow it had to bleed, and bleed a lot. That hadn't happened enough with the frame, and the nail would assist in creating the pressure that would cause the blood to flow. Of course, he reminded me gravely, there was still no guarantee it would work. If it didn't, they might have to remove the unresponsive section altogether and graft a piece of bone from my hip. That would mean having my leg back in a frame so we could begin to regrow the bone all over again – and that would take months.

The thought was appalling. Back in June I'd been sure we were over this hurdle. Dinesh was pulling no punches;

every wound, injury, every smashed leg is different, and my break was as bad as a break could get. He made it clear that a bone graft was a step we might have to take, but it wasn't the next step; first we'd see how the nail fared. I asked him what would happen if none of this treatment worked. He told me they would have no option but to amputate the leg.

I could barely believe my ears. All this time, all this effort with the frame and crutches, the walking stick and Exogen machine, and I still might lose my leg. Deep down, I was terrified. June was supposed to have been D-Day – and yet here we were all over again. I was so pissed off I went to the annual Movember charity lunch and got really drunk. That helped for a while, but not much.

As I contemplated this next operation, I made a conscious decision not to think too far ahead. There was no point – the whole recovery process was just too big. I told myself to take this in bite-size chunks. It's what I'd been doing all along, and it was more important than ever to keep doing it now; the next stage was all I could cope with. I concentrated on the positives. A nail would stabilise my leg and allow me to be much more mobile much more quickly, and there was no reason it would not work. If it did, I'd be on my feet and fully bearing my own weight in a matter of days, and could be back on a motorbike in six weeks.

I wanted some reassurance, and much as Olly had been my rock through everything, there's only so much you can ask of one person. So, of course, I called my dad.

After I'd explained what the surgeon had said, Dad told me to stay positive and started reminding me of all the different experiences and challenges I'd faced in my life – like the time when he took some of his more controversial films to show in South Africa. It was back in the worst days of Apartheid, when the political upheaval there was on the news every night, and the country was boycotted by much of the arts community.

Dad took me with him for some father-and-son time. I was about seven or eight at the time, and I remember being really excited. But when I got there I was shocked. My parents were the kind of people who embraced society as a whole, and I had no idea what prejudice was until I arrived in South Africa. I couldn't believe that black people had to walk on one side of the street in Johannesburg and Cape Town while whites were on the other. We travelled downtown in a bus and the black people were not only segregated – the buses were split with wire mesh.

While we were there we hooked up with this farmer who invited us to stay with him for a couple of days. His farm was so big he moved about in a plane – a single-engine Cessna. He took us up one day with Dad in the back and me in the co-pilot's seat, and I had to kneel up just so I could see out of the windscreen. About 20 minutes into the flight the farmer turned to me and indicated a dial on the dash where a little plane was displayed. With a wink at my dad he said, 'Charley, I need to turn around for a bit and talk to your father. That means you'll have to take the stick and keep an eye on that gauge there on the dash.'

I stared, incredulous. 'You…you want me to fly the plane?'

'Sure, all you have to do is hold the stick and keep an eye on the sky as well as that airplane gauge. See the way it moves? You need to keep the wings in line. OK?'

With that, he left me to it. He and Dad chatted away and I was on my knees reminded of being in Dad's car at home with Daisy when we drove into the ditch. But this wasn't a car, it was a plane; and I was only seven years old. For ten minutes or so I held onto that stick, my jaws grinding together, sweat beading in my hair, hands white at the knuckle. I felt giddy and sick but kept my gaze flitting between what I could see through the windscreen and that gauge. I was determined to keep the wings where they were supposed to be. I was determined to fly the plane.

I did that for as long as I could but, finally, I couldn't take it. Still gripping the stick with both hands, I turned to the farmer. 'I can't do this anymore,' I said. 'You'll have to take over. I can't hold on any longer.'

'Alright,' he said and swivelled around in the seat. With one hand on my shoulder, he told me how well I'd done – then flipped the switch to disengage the autopilot.

Dad recalled that day when we were on the phone, telling me that it had been a bit of fun for him and the farmer but he'd also seen the concentration, the determination on my face. He told me it was that kind of grit I needed now. Another operation, another phase in my recovery – this thing with the 'intramedullary nail' was just the next step.

OUT OF THE BENDS
AND INTO THE
STRAIGHT

The nail went in on 30 November, and almost immediately I began to feel better. Within a couple of days I had dispensed with the crutches and was walking with just my cane. Time, that had seemed to pass so slowly whilst I was incapacitated, started to speed up again.

My next appointment was on 16 December, and the surgeon was really pleased with my progress. He trimmed the stitches and told me he was happy with the way the nail had aligned and the fact I was putting plenty of weight on my leg. It was too early to see any real progress around the fracture site itself, but I was moving much more easily now and had enough freedom in my ankle to consider changing gear on a motorbike.

God, I could almost taste it, the freedom I'd been denied for nearly a year. That said, given the severity of the break I was actually pretty lucky. Not long after I was back from the hospital I bumped into a GP in the local supermarket, and

he told me that so many people in my position had to
endure the frame for two years or more. When he saw me
with just a cane he was amazed at the rate of my progress. That
was hugely encouraging. I'd been pretty upbeat since the last
operation but to hear something like that from another
doctor was a real bonus.

The new year was on my mind and I was determined to
be back on a bike before the anniversary of the accident. My
eldest daughter Doone turned 21 on 21 December – another
milestone. I could barely believe it; all grown up, and Kinvara
was 19 already too. This past year had felt like I'd seen more
of the girls than in a dozen previous years put together.
Birthdays, Christmas…these dates suddenly seemed like
landmarks. I really was beginning to feel as if I was coming
out of the last few bends and into the home straight, finally.

The more I thought about it, the more my bike senses
seemed to be heightened. I could smell the tarmac just after
it rained. I could feel the dust of the roads in Africa. I could
see the way the sun slants across the landscape in those first
few hours of the morning, when to be on a bike is to be in
heaven. I could feel the crisp winter air on a cold, cold day,
the tyres skating a little as I shift my weight on the seat.

The threat to my leg was still there, but I was confident
the nail would work, and, as the weeks passed, it did seem to
feel much stronger. Whether that was the bone regrouping
properly or the nail, only time would tell, but for now at
least the moment when I would be out of the bends and
into that last home straight was getting closer and closer.

I was conscious of that episode with the moped, of course, caused by my craving to get riding as soon as possible. I was so lucky then, but it did nothing to temper my desire. As the new year approached I was desperate to go outside and get on the silver Kawasaki W650 I customised with Roy. A little like me, it's been chained up for a year. Every time I shuffle past I can almost hear it spitting and snarling at me. It's got this amazing lightweight one-piece titanium exhaust made by Racefit that I can lift with my pinky finger and sounds awesome. Though the lithium battery was flat after a year of inactivity, I knew it was that bike I'd be riding just as soon as I was able.

But I couldn't get ahead of myself. I wasn't there yet — though for the first time since the accident, I really knew I would be. So much had happened, and I'd had so much time to think and reflect when normally I'd be so active. It was that sense of anticipation, of approaching activity, that kept me going. There had been some dark days, weeks, months even; but now I felt I was at the beginning of the end. I just needed to pace myself. If I could carry on with the physio and keep working on the exercise bicycle I'd be strong and confident enough, when the time felt right, to throw my leg over the saddle.

Confidence; it's played a massive part in my life, and this is the first opportunity I've had to really consider it. I needed one last shot of it for the final push and as the strength began to return to my leg, I had it. I could feel it grow and grow as the days passed and Christmas approached. It was as if a switch had been thrown in my psyche. I thrive on confidence a lot more than most people maybe, and that's all to do with motorbikes. Self-assurance with perhaps a hint of arrogance is essential in any serious rider, and though I'm not the racer I might've have been, motorcycles have been my life.

When Christmas was over, Olly and I drove to Scotland to spend Hogmanay with Shaun and Joanna MacDonald. They're old, old friends of ours; we saw them in the summer when my leg was still very much encased in the frame, and we were really looking forward to a few freezing days on Black Isle. (I'm not sure why they call it Black 'Isle' because it's not an island but a peninsula. There's water on three sides, the Cromarty Firth to the north, Beauly to the south and Moray to the east, and when we were there in the summer the weather had been spectacular.)

On the drive north we talked about all that had happened in the past year, and Olly suggested that in many ways it had been a journey of self-discovery.

'It's allowed your mind to work in a way it's not really had to before,' she told me. 'You've had the chance to look back on all you've achieved and use it as a spur to forge a new path.'

I'd never thought of it quite like that, but she was right. Normally I'm so busy exploring far-flung corners of the globe on a motorbike, I forget that life can be quieter and more reflective. The time spent sitting at home working on this book, talking to my dad, my sisters and my wife, has offered me a fresh perspective. The memories I've shared with you, all the way back to those early days in Annamoe when confidence exuded from every pore in my body – it occurred to me then that this past year had been a coming-of-age I hadn't thought possible, or even necessary. I'd been forced to consider a life without motorbikes and face the biggest test someone in my position could ever encounter.

They say that how you deal with a major setback in your life is when you find out who you really are. There's no doubt that's true, and as the moment when I'd be able to ride again grew closer, all that I'd learned about myself seemed ever more apparent. Life is a moveable feast and if we allow ourselves the opportunity we can become more accomplished with every pothole we encounter in the road. Time flies by so fast and life is over in the blink of an eye; I'd learned how important it is to make the most of any opportunity. I'd come through this year more aware than I was before. I understood who I was and who I would be better than I could have imagined.

We were joined for New Year by Sean Kelly, an old friend of ours who just happens to be a knee specialist. I've known him a long time, and at 3am on New Year's Day he was vigorously massaging my leg. When I say vigorous, it was intense – working the shin and calf, beating up on my knee like you wouldn't believe. If he had been anything other than a surgeon I'd have called the massage an assault, but he knows what he's doing and really worked on the muscles. The fact that it seemed to take such a pummelling without too much distress was a good sign, though in the morning it felt pretty tender.

Back home in London I had a quiet month to look forward to. As I said, we'd decided to put the tours on hold until a 'Ride with Charley Boorman' meant just that, instead of having him along by way of Skype. This year there was no Australian tour and we'd postponed planning any others in South America as well. I called Ewan to wish him a happy New Year and we talked for a while. Later in the month he would be in London for the release of *T2: Trainspotting*, 20 years after the first film was made. I had my fingers crossed that it would do really well. Ewan was back in Scotland playing a Scottish lad again, albeit all grown up, and working again with Danny Boyle – after all these years it had been something of a homecoming.

Talking to him reminded me of the day at Victoria Falls back in 2007 when riding a motorbike from John O'Groats to Cape Town wasn't enough, and I had to tie a piece of elastic to my ankles and plummet from 100 metres above the Zambezi. I'm 50 years old now – I was almost 40 then – but I'd do that bungee jump again if my left leg would support it. It's who I am, and I remember Ewan (who's always been a little more circumspect) telling me how just watching it had made him feel sick.

I'd survived the jump and we'd got back on the bikes with just the final few days of that mammoth trip to go. The memories and the miles behind us played through my head as clearly as they do now; those baking African roads, powering on with the coast on our left and the desert on our right; the long expanses as we crossed Libya under government escort, sand drifting treacherously across the tarmac. Another journey coming to an end – only back then the finish line was climbing from the saddle for the last time after thousands of miles, and now it was throwing a leg over a saddle for the first time in a year.

Fingers crossed, I was over the hump, and riding in Africa was my new goal. Perhaps it would be a slightly different Charley on that tour come September 2017, but I was aiming to be fit both physically and emotionally. The original target of crossing the Darien Gap hadn't been shelved – it was merely on hold. That wasn't solely down to my leg; it was also to do with the weather. There is only one real window of opportunity for the Gap and that's around February of each year, when the rivers and ravines are just about passable.

Africa was a much more realistic target. From Cape Town to the Victoria Falls; Zimbabwe, Botswana, and then back into South Africa and Lesotho through the infamous Sani Pass, a dirt road that weaves through the Drakensberg Mountains at an elevation of over 2,800 metres. It's one of the most amazing rides any biker can undertake and I'm grateful I've been able to introduce a few people to it. Africa had extra significance for me too. The path I've been on for the last decade or so all started with Ewan and me, and the first time I'd ridden that part of the world was with Ewan in 2007. By the time I rode there again ten years would have passed, and that felt like an important anniversary.

I missed being on those adventures. I missed the challenge and the people. I missed working for UNICEF. I really value my work with them; I've been privileged to have seen the amazing things they do and I've missed the faces of the children. Mongolia, Africa, all points in between; the enthusiasm and hope these kids have never ceases to astound me, whether they're the victims of land mines or famine, or fighting wars as child soldiers. No matter how low they've been brought I always sense something indomitable about them. A powerful will to not only survive but prosper, to overcome the odds and – metaphorically at least – get back on the bike. That spirit has rubbed off on me over the years.

It was on my mind as I spent my time getting these last few thoughts on the page. All my books so far have been about the journey, the road and the elements, and the people I've met on the way. This has been a different kind of journey; hopefully, by the time you've finished reading, you'll know a little bit more about how my life has shaped the guy you've met on tour or seen on TV.

I realise now that this whole year has not just been about getting back on a motorbike, but about getting back to my way of life. Long Way Back: that's exactly what it has been. In revisiting my past I've tried to figure out, for myself as much as you guys, what it is that makes me tick. I've always been driven by a thirst for adventure in this race of life I've found myself involved in. After a childhood with parents who never settled for anything less than the fulfilment of their dreams, I'm immensely grateful to both my mum and my dad. They taught me to follow my heart, to overcome the obstacles of life with a smile on my face and a level of pragmatism that isn't given to being overly emotional. Didn't Kipling write a poem about triumph and disaster? How you can watch things break that you gave your life to, then build them up with worn-out tools? That's how this last year feels, literally from Triumph to disaster – I'll never forget my orthopaedic surgeon and that box of ancient tools!

Motorbikes have been my life, and that passion seems to have struck a chord with people in a way that's been life-affirming for me. Hopefully some of what I've done has inspired others to take up this two-wheeled adventure. I know the tours we started in South Africa have enabled a whole raft of people from different parts of the world and a plethora of backgrounds to discover that, far from being daunting and dangerous, that part of the world is as welcoming as it is incredible. It's not just the road, but those you share the journey with. If I've learned one thing during this year of inactivity, it's to appreciate the people who've been there for me. My wife is still the rock she's always been throughout our quarter of a century of marriage. She's the pragmatist, the one who has thought through every twist and turn, looking well beyond the next corner in the style of Valentino Rossi. She's nursed me without complaint, taken the brunt of my moods when things weren't going well and dealt with the additional, self-inflicted moments of potential catastrophe. I'm lucky to have her.

Leaning on my cane, I hobbled outside to take a long look at the Kawasaki. The more I looked, the more I was yearning to be on it again, even if it was just pootling up and down our quiet road to practise getting my left foot under the gear shifter. I realised the last time I changed gear on a motorbike was in Portugal as I stepped down to overtake that Mercedes. I thought about Hutchy having to re-learn his skills all over again, having to use his right foot instead of his left. As I pictured it I was suddenly back at Brands Hatch on Ewan's old 748 with my knee on the tarmac coming out of Clark Curve. Under the bridge and onto the rise, then a long, long right, knee on the floor and the throttle pretty much pinned, the back end stepping out in the kind of slide that leaves big black lines of rubber. God I missed it, the way the hairs on your arms stand up and your cheeks prickle with the rush of adrenaline.

It wasn't just the track I missed; it was weaving through London traffic. Every gap taken, going where cars cannot go, accelerating hard only to slam on the brakes to the point where the rear wheel is off the ground in a stoppie. Emotionally I was flying. That old slip road in Slough where I used to crank it hard to the left, the roundabout at Shepherd's Bush where I first touched my knee down. The Road of Bones in Siberia. Libya in the middle of a sandstorm, passing an old wreck of a car that came lumbering up the wrong side of the road while lorries with no lights appeared from the haze and summoned a blast of wind that rattled the bikes as we passed. I remember the stench of rubbish in the air and thinking how it wasn't any fun...but as I stood there staring at my W650, all I could think about was how great it would be to ride that storm again negotiating the panicked traffic.

With every day that passed now I would test my leg more and more. I'd apply a little more weight, intensify the physio and ride the exercise bicycle as if my life depended upon it. Every night I would lie on my back and stare at the ceiling, conscious of every breath with the kind of heightened sense of anticipation I'd experienced on the dunes I rode in the Dakar. My mouth would dry out. I'd hear every movement around me, be aware of the slightest changes in temperature. I'd try to sleep but sleep wouldn't come, and I'd be back in the sand with the bike almost drowning and somehow staying upright. I'd hit gravel with the heat in my face and sweat burning my eyes, the breath so tight in my chest it wasn't oxygen but dust I was breathing. I'd feel the back end step out and the front almost fold and I'd compensate, correct each undulation the trail would throw at me, sitting down or standing on the pegs with my elbows out and my hands soft as the miles slipped by beneath me.

I'd lie there thinking about the twisting, turning gravel of the Ethiopian highlands from *Long Way Down*. Soaked and slick with rain, 500 feet of sheer drop to one side or the other and no barrier to get in the way. Rockfalls and mudslides tested us further; I had to jump one massive slide with both wheels off the ground, then screw the back end around like a speedway rider just to stop myself sliding over the cliff edge and vanishing into oblivion.

Sitting up in bed I'd look down at my sleeping wife with a hint of sweat on my brow as I relived those moments over and over again. There was nothing melancholy about it, no pang of remorse for what had been, only excitement for what lay ahead. I still didn't know how long it would take to get back to where I'd been – but I didn't have to race the TT, I just had to race myself.

I remembered back in 2007 as Ewan and I navigated the Skeleton Coast in Namibia with Cape Town and the finish line just ahead. Mountains breaking up the horizon, the road nothing but a painted ribbon of dirt that cut through a landscape of sand and cactus, vast and empty. We stopped on the beach to look at the wreck of some old fishing vessel that rocked back and forth in the breakers where it had been trapped quite close to the shore. The way the hull rolled in the surf, how the waves pushed and pulled its progress; I couldn't help but compare it to the year I'd been through. Almost there but not quite, almost free only to be set back again and again. Perhaps that ship was still there, perhaps it had broken up, but one thing was for sure: it never sailed again. Would I sail again? For almost a year I'd lived with the threat of my way of life being broken to pieces. The truth is that even as I write this, until the surgeons tell me I have a fully functional tibia again, that threat still remains. But as each day goes by the threat is less and less.

Over the next few days I was visited by so many memories of being on a bike and the emotions those journeys carried, it almost swamped me. Somebody was telling me something. Some inner voice. It's time, Charley. It's time.

On Friday 6 January I took the battery off the W650 and put it on charge. Saturday morning dawned dull and damp and I hobbled downstairs. Grabbing the bike keys, I lifted my helmet from the peg and threw on a jacket then went out to the drive.

The moment was upon me, and Olly seemed to sense it even before I told her what I planned to do. She came outside and we didn't say anything. I just looked at her and she looked at me as I leant on my cane. I still wasn't walking on my own, but the inability to walk never stopped any racer getting on a motorbike. I was tingling, physically shaking. I could feel sweat on my palm as I worked the keys in my hand then bent to unlock the chain. Finally, my helmet was down over my ears and I fitted the key in the ignition

I stood there not quite believing I was doing this – the moped was one thing, but this was a full-blown gear-shifting motorbike. As I reached for the handlebars I hesitated. I could feel my sister Telsche. It was as if she was standing right next to me, and I hadn't felt her presence so strongly in quite some time. It was so intense it seemed like all I had to do was look round and I would see her. Swallowing hard, a lump in my throat, I gripped the bars with both hands and wheeled the bike around. Then – finally – I lifted my leg over the saddle.

I sat there for a few seconds recalling how whenever I rode, wherever I rode, Telsche was always with me. She was with me now. I pressed the starter and the engine kicked into life. A twist of the wrist and the rasp crackled from the titanium exhaust pipe. I looked over my shoulder as I pressed my foot on the lever and clicked into first gear. Olly was there beside me as my gaze shifted to the windowsill of our living room, and the bronze of my sister's perfect hands. There was a peace about them, a silence. For a moment, the world was so still I could almost hear her whisper. Cracking the throttle again I could see her smile as I pulled out onto the road.

In memory of

My mother Christel and my sister Telsche

Still such a massive part of my life.
I think about them every day.

ACKNOWLEDGEMENTS

I'd like to thank Robert Kirby, who made this happen
Jeff Gulvin, who helped me collect my thoughts
Helen Brocklehurst and Rebecca Needes,
who bought into the idea

and

David Kent, who's been part of the ride
since *Long Way Round*.

★

I'd like to offer my appreciation to Jon Simmons and
Dinesh Nathwani, two of the finest surgeons in London.

★

Finally,

I'd like to give special thanks to my dad John
and my sisters, Katrine and Daisy, who reminded
me of so much on the way.

unicef

Unicef has been making the world a safer place for children for over 70 years. In that time, we've done more to influence laws, policies and customs that help protect children than anyone else.

When children face wars, disease, exploitation and disasters, we're there. Unicef works in more countries than any other children's organization, so whenever and wherever children need us most, we can reach them – often faster than anyone else. Thanks to our life-saving food and clean water, our temporary hospitals and our vaccines, children are surviving. They're going to the schools we've helped build, they're taught by teachers we've helped train, and they're listened to by counsellors we've supported.

Unicef is the only children's organisation named in the UN Convention on the Rights of the Child. And we hold governments to the promises they've made to look after our children.

Unicef gets things done. And with your help, we will reach every child in danger.

The Movember Foundation is the only charity tackling men's health on a global scale, year round. By 2030, Movember aims to reduce the number of men dying prematurely by 25%.

The Foundation funds game-changing men's health projects. Millions have joined the movement, raising £443M to help to fund over 1,200 projects focusing on prostate cancer, testicular cancer, mental health and suicide prevention.

In addition, Movember's Awareness and Education programme is encouraging men to become more aware of their health, to talk about the big stuff in life, and take action when health issues arise.

Our fathers, partners, brothers and friends face a health crisis that isn't being talked about. We can't afford to stay silent. Movember Foundation has one goal: to stop men dying too young.